Meditations
on the
Divine Liturgy

Meditations
on the
Divine Liturgy

of the
Holy Eastern Orthodox Catholic
and Apostolic Church

Nikolai Gogol

Translated by L. Alexieff

Edited by Archimandrite Lazarus

Updated and Revised 3rd Edition

Holy Trinity Publications
The Printshop of St Job of Pochaev
Holy Trinity Monastery
Jordanville, New York
2014

Printed with the blessing of His Eminence,
Metropolitan Hilarion, First Hierarch
of the Russian Orthodox Church Outside of Russia

Meditations on the Divine Liturgy–3rd Edition © 2014
Holy Trinity Monastery

Second Printing 2021

HOLY TRINITY PUBLICATIONS
The Printshop of St Job of Pochaev
Holy Trinity Monastery
Jordanville, New York 13361-0036
www.holytrinitypublications.com

Third Edition ISBN: 978-0-88465-343-1 (paperback)
ISBN: 978-0-88465-362-2 (ePub)
ISBN: 978-0-88465-364-6 (Mobipocket)

Library of Congress Control Number 2013952604

CONTENTS

Nikolai Vasilievich Gogol (1809–1852)

INTRODUCTION

The Divine Liturgy is the eternal repetition of the great act of love accomplished for us. Suffering from the ramifications of the fall, mankind cried out from all the ends of the earth to its Creator. Those living in the darkness of idolatry and without the knowledge of God heard that order and harmony could be restored only by Him Who had ordered the worlds He had created to move in unison. From everywhere, yearning creation cried out to its Creator. Everything sent up cries of grief to the Author of its being, and these cries were more perceptibly heard on the lips of the elect and the prophets. They foretold and realized that if the Creator should Himself stand face to face with men, He would not do so otherwise than in the form of His creation, whom He had created in His own image and likeness. The Incarnation of God on earth was comprehended by all mankind only in as far their understanding of God had been purified. But no one proclaimed this truth so clearly as the prophets of

God's chosen people. Whilst even the pagans had presentiments of His Incarnation from the immaculate Virgin, nowhere was it foreseen with such palpable clarity as by the prophets.

The cries were heard. He Who had made the world appeared in the world. He appeared among us in the form of a man like ourselves, as had been dimly foretold even in the deep darkness of paganism, but not in such a way as unpurified minds had imagined. Not as a king in proud splendor and pomp, not as a chastiser of wrongs, not as a judge come to destroy some and reward others. No! A brother's gentle kiss was heard. He made His appearance as only God could have done, just as the prophets who had received the command from God had portrayed Him.

The Office of Preparation

The Proskomedia[1]

The priest who intends to celebrate the Liturgy should be abstinent in body and spirit from the previous evening, should be at peace with all, and should avoid holding a grudge towards anyone. From the evening on, after reading the prescribed prayers, he should dwell with his mind in the altar, (sanctuary)[2] thinking of the morrow's duties so that even his very thoughts may be duly consecrated and filled with sweet fragrance. When the time comes, he goes to the church with the deacon; together they bow before the holy doors and then kiss the icons of the Saviour and of the Mother of God, after which they bow to all present, by this bow asking forgiveness of everyone. Then they go into the altar, reciting to themselves the Psalm:

I shall go into Thy house; I shall worship toward Thy holy temple in fear of Thee. Ps 5:7 (DLJC p. 13)[*]

---

[*]From John Chrysostom, *The Divine Liturgy of Our Father Among the Saints* (DLJC), Slavonic-English Parallel Text, 3rd ed. (Jordanville, N.Y.: Holy Trinity Publications, 2013), p. 13. Note: all further quotations from this text will be marked as DLJC p. *x*.

Approaching the holy table itself, they turn towards the East and make three prostrations, and kiss the holy table and the Book of the Gospels lying on it as if it were the Lord Himself sitting on the throne. Then they put on their sacred vestments in order to be distinguished not only from others but even from themselves, so that there may be nothing in their appearance to remind people of men engaged in the everyday affairs of the world. At the same time, this should put them in mind of the grandeur of the service which is about to begin.

From Apostolic times, special vestments were in use, although the persecuted Church was not in a position to give them the beauty we are accustomed to. But from the very beginning there were strict rules that the priest must not serve in his ordinary clothing, and that none of the clergy should walk in the street in the vestments worn during church services. While they are putting on these bright vestments, the servants of the Church are obliged to clothe themselves also in the robes of the Spirit. For this reason, as each article is put on, verses from the Psalms are recited which disclose the deep meaning of the vestments, so that the thoughts of the clergy may not wander while they are doing something so simple and ordinary as dressing. Rather, even while vesting they collect themselves for their high service and like Aaron, splendidly clad both externally and in spirit, they step before the dread altar of the Most High.

Priest and deacon, taking their vestments in their hands, make three bows towards the East and repeat silently:

O God, cleanse me a sinner, and have mercy on me. (DLJC p. 15)

The deacon takes his sticharion and orarion and asks the priest to bless them. Upon receiving the blessing, he goes aside and vests. First, he puts on the sticharion, which is of a bright color, signifying the radiant attire of the angels and calling to mind the unsullied purity of heart that ought to be inseparable from the priestly office. The deacon and priest, after putting on their sticharia say:

My soul shall rejoice in the Lord, for He hath clothed me in the garment of salvation, and with the vesture of gladness hath He covered me; He hath placed a crown upon me as on a bridegroom, and He hath adorned me as a bride with comeliness. Isa 61:10 (DLJC p. 15)

Then the deacon kisses his orarion, a long narrow band, and hangs it over his left shoulder. The orarion is the symbol of the office of deacon: with it the deacon gives the sign for the commencement of every part of the church service—for the worshippers to pray, the choir to sing, the priest to begin his duties, and for the deacon himself to have the swiftness of the angels and their readiness to serve. The office of deacon corresponds to that of the angels in heaven. According to the interpretation of St John Chrysostom, this narrow band on the deacon's shoulder fluttering to and fro like a wing symbolizes the flying of the angels. Next, the deacon puts on cuffs, which are fastened firmly about the wrists so as to allow the hands greater freedom of movement and dexterity during the sacred office. While putting them on, he meditates on the all-creative and omnipresent power of God. For the right cuff, he recites:

> **Thy right hand, O Lord, is glorified in strength; Thy right hand, O Lord, hath shattered enemies, and in the multitude of Thy glory hast Thou ground down the adversaries. Exod 15:6–7** (DLJC p. 15)

As he puts on the left cuff, he reflects that he is the work of God's hands, and asks his Creator to direct him with His guidance from above, saying:

> **Thy hands have made me and fashioned me; give me understanding and I will learn Thy commandments. Ps 119:73** (DLJC p. 16)

The priest vests in a similar manner. First, he blesses his sticharion and puts it on while reciting the same words the deacon recited. Then, instead of a simple, plain orarion on one shoulder, he puts on a double orarion that covers both shoulders and goes round the neck, joining in front and reaching to the hem of his clothes, indicating by this union the twofold nature of his office, that of priest and deacon. As the name *epitrachelion*[3] (that is, "on the neck") implies, it signifies the outpouring of grace from above on the priest; hence, he recites these sublime words from Scripture:

Blessed is God Who poureth out His grace upon His priests, like unto the oil of myrrh upon the head, which runneth down upon the beard, upon the beard of Aaron, which runneth down to the fringe of his raiment. Ps 133:2 (DLJC p. 19)

Using the same words as the deacon, he puts on the cuffs, and then the belt over his sticharion and epitrachelion, so that during the holy office he will not be inconvenienced by the looseness of the vestments. Moreover, this girding attests to his readiness for service, for a man girds himself when he sets out on a journey or undertakes an important task. So, too, the priest girds himself when he sets about his heavenly ministry, and regarding his belt as the strength of divine power that strengthens him, he recites:

Blessed is God Who girded me with power, and hath made my path blameless, Who maketh my feet like the feet of a hart, and setteth me upon high places. [That is, the house of the Lord.] Ps 18:32–33 (DLJC p. 19)

If he belongs to the higher clergy, he hangs at his left side the oblong epigonation, which denotes the Sword of the Spirit, the all-conquering power of the Divine Word, proclaiming the unceasing struggle that man faces in this world to declare the victory that Christ gained over death so that man's immortal spirit might struggle courageously against its corruption. That is why the epigonation has the appearance of a mighty weapon and is hung on the thigh where man's strength lies. Meanwhile, this prayer is being recited:

> **Gird Thy sword upon Thy thigh, O Mighty One, in Thy comeliness and Thy beauty, and bend Thy bow, and proceed prosperously, and be king, because of truth and meekness and righteousness, and Thy right hand shall guide Thee wondrously, always, now and ever, and unto the ages of ages. Amen. Ps 45:3–5** (DLJC p. 19)

Finally, the priest completes his vesting by putting on the phelonion, the uppermost vestment, covering all the others and symbolizing the all-embracing justice of God, and says:

> **Thy priests, O Lord, shall be clothed with righteousness, and Thy saints with rejoicing shall rejoice, always, now and ever, and unto the ages of ages. Amen. Ps 132:9** (DLJC p. 20)

Thus invested with the divine instruments, the priest is now another man. Whatever he may be as an individual, however unworthy of his vocation, everyone present in the church looks upon him as God's instrument, through whom the Holy Spirit works. The priest and deacon then wash their hands, saying from the Psalm:

I will wash my hands in innocence and I will compass Thine altar, O Lord. Ps 26:6 (DLJC p. 21)

Then they make three bows to the waist with the words:

O God, cleanse me a sinner and have mercy on me. (DLJC p. 23)

They are now cleansed and enlightened, like their shining vestments. They no longer remind us of ordinary people, but resemble radiant visions rather than men.

The deacon reminds the priest to begin the divine service with the words: **Bless, master** (DLJC p. 23), and the priest begins with the words:

Blessed is our God, always, now and ever, and to the ages of ages, (DLJC p. 23)

and goes to the table of oblation at the side. This entire part of the service consists of the preparation of what is needed for the service, that is, the removal from the prosphoron that portion which at first must represent the body of Christ and later be changed into It. The table at the side, to the left of the altar, called the prothesis (that is, "table of offering or preparation," because on it the loaves are prepared), represents the place in the early Church where everything that the early Christians brought for the service and for their common meal was kept.

Because the whole **proskomedia** is nothing more than a preparation for the Liturgy itself, the Church has connected it with the commemoration of the early life of Christ, which was a preparation for His public ministry. All this is carried out in the altar behind closed doors and drawn curtain, unseen by the congregation, just as Christ's early life was hidden from the masses. But for the worshippers during this time, the **Hours** are read, a collection of Psalms and prayers that the early Christians read at the four most important times of the day: the First Hour, when the day begins, according to the Church's reckoning; the Third Hour, when the Holy Spirit descended; the Sixth Hour, when the Saviour of the world was nailed to the cross; and the Ninth Hour, when He yielded up His spirit. Because present-day Christians, owing to lack of time and constant distractions, cannot read these prayers at the appointed times, they are read one after the other at this time.[4]

The priest goes to the table of oblation and takes up one of the prosphora in order to remove that part which will afterwards become the Body of Christ—the center with the seal bearing the name of Jesus Christ. This removal of bread from bread represents the separation of Christ's flesh from the flesh of the Virgin—the birth of the Fleshless One in the flesh. And reflecting that this is the birth of the One Who offered Himself as a sacrifice for the whole world, the priest inevitably connects the thought of the sacrifice itself with the offering and regards the bread as the "Lamb" offered in sacrifice; the spear, with which he will cut it out, as the sacrificial knife—a reminder of the spear with which the Saviour's body was pierced on the cross.

At this point the priest does not accompany his acts with the Saviour's words or with the words of the eye-witnesses, the contemporaries who lived through all these events. He does not transport himself in mind back to the time when the historical offering of this sacrifice took place, for all this is presented in the latter part of the Liturgy. For the moment, he is in the even more distant past looking ahead to what is to come (that is, to the coming of the Messiah).

Like the people who sat in darkness and saw a great light, he looks towards the light beaming ahead of him. As Isaiah foresaw with the eagle eye of prophetic vision what was to come after his time, just so the priest through this proskomedia looks prophetically to the sacrificial act ahead of him. Uniting himself with the prophet, he accompanies each ritual act with the words of the Prophet Isaiah, who foresaw out of ages of darkness the wondrous Birth, Sacrifice, and Death and proclaimed it with unbelievable clarity. The priest thrusts the spear into the right side of the seal and says:

He is led as a sheep to the slaughter. Isa 53:7 (DLJC p. 23)

And then thrusting it into the left side he says:

> **And as a blameless lamb before his shearer is dumb, so He openeth not his mouth. Isa 53:7** (DLJC p. 25)

Then thrusting the spear into the upper part of the seal he says:

> **In His lowliness His judgment was taken away. Isa 53:8** (DLJC p. 25)

Finally, thrusting it into the lower part, he pronounces the words of the prophet who was absorbed in contemplation of the wondrous origin or lineage of the condemned Lamb:

> **And who shall declare his generation? Isa 53:8** (DLJC p. 25)

With the spear he lifts out the portion of bread cut out of the center and says:

> **For His life is taken away from the earth. Isa 53: 8** (DLJC p. 25)

Turning this portion of the seal downwards, he now cuts it cross-wise as a sign of His death on the cross and says:

> **Sacrificed is the Lamb of God, that taketh away the sin of the world, for the life and salvation of the world. John 1:29; 1 John 2:2** (DLJC p. 27)

Then the priest thrusts the spear into the right side as a reminder of the offering of the sacrifice, of how the soldier at the cross pierced our Saviour's side, and says:

One of the soldiers with a spear pierced His side, and forthwith there came out blood and water. And he who saw it bare record, and his record is true. John 19:34-35 (DLJC p. 27)

At the same time, these words are the sign for the deacon to pour wine and water into the holy chalice. The deacon reverently observes all that the priest does, and prompts him to begin each ritual act by saying: **Let us pray to the Lord** (DLJC p. 25). Finally, he pours wine and water into the chalice, after mixing them and asking the priest's blessing. The wine and bread are prepared in this way so they may be changed later during the sublime action of the Liturgy that lies ahead.

Then, following the ritual of the early Church and the holy Christians of the first century—who, whenever they thought of Christ, always remembered all those who had been nearest to His heart through the fulfillment of His commandments and by the holiness of their lives—the priest takes the other prosphora in order to cut out of them portions in their memory and place them on the diskos, or paten, beside the "Lamb," or holy bread that represents the Lord Himself, since they themselves had a burning desire to be everywhere with their Lord.

Taking into his hand the second prosphoron, he cuts out of it a portion in honor and memory of our most blessed Lady, the Mother of God and Ever-Virgin Mary, and places it on the right of the "Lamb," pronouncing the prophetic verse from the Psalm:

At Thy right hand stood the Queen, arrayed in a vesture of in woven gold, adorned in varied colors. Ps 44:10
(DLJC p. 31)

Then he takes the third prosphoron in memory of the saints and with the spear removes nine portions in three rows of three each. The first is in memory of John the Baptist; the second, of the prophets; the third, of the apostles; this concludes the first row and the first group of saints. Then he cuts out a fourth portion for the holy fathers and prelates, a fifth for the martyrs, and a sixth for the holy and God-bearing fathers and mothers; this concludes the second row and the second group of saints. The seventh is in memory of wonder-working unmercenaries or doctors who took no fees; the eighth, of the ancestors of our Lord, Joachim and Anna, and of the saint whose day it is; the ninth of St John Chrysostom or St Basil the Great, depending on which liturgy is being celebrated; thus concluding the third row and the third group of saints. All these nine portions are placed on the diskos to the left of the holy bread or "Lamb" (the priest's right). So Christ appears amongst His nearest and dearest; He Who dwells in His saints is seen visibly among them—God among the gods, a Man among men.

From the fourth prosphoron, the priest removes portions for all the living: for all rulers, for Orthodox patriarchs and bishops,

for the Holy Synod, for the reigning emperor and all his house, and for all Orthodox Christians. He then takes out particles for all persons whom he desires to mention by name or whom he has been requested to commemorate.

Finally, the priest takes the last prosphoron and removes from it particles in memory of the departed, praying at the same time for the remission of their sins, commencing with the patriarchs, the emperors, the founders of the church in which he is celebrating, the bishop who ordained him if he is among the departed, and continuing on to the humblest of the faithful. He mentions those whom he has been requested to commemorate, and those whom he himself wishes to remember. At the end, he prays for the forgiveness of his own sins and removes a particle on behalf of himself. All these particles in memory of the persons mentioned are placed on the diskos below the "Lamb." So around this holy bread, this "Lamb" symbolizing Christ

Himself, is collected His entire Church—triumphant in heaven and militant here on earth. The Son of Man appears amongst men, for whose sake He was incarnate and became man. Then the priest takes the sponge and carefully collects with it all the crumbs on the diskos, so that no fragment of the holy bread should be lost. The particles removed for those who offered the breads and for those for whom they were offered are, at the end of the liturgy, placed into the chalice, with the prayer:

By Thy precious Blood O Lord, wash away the sins of those here commemorated, through the intercessions of Thy saints. (DLJC p. 187)

After leaving the table of oblation, the priest bows as if to the Incarnate Christ Himself and acknowledges in the form of the bread laying on the diskos the appearance of the Heavenly Bread on earth. And he censes it with holy incense, after blessing the incense and saying the prayer:

Incense do we offer unto Thee, O Christ our God, as an odor of spiritual fragrance; accepting it upon Thy most heavenly altar, do Thou send down upon us the grace of Thy Most-holy Spirit. (DLJC p. 43)

Transporting himself in thought to the time of Christ's birth and turning the past into the present, the priest regards the table of oblation as the secret cave in which heaven was then transferred to earth. Heaven became a cave, and a cave became heaven. Having censed the asterisk, or star-cover, and placed it over the diskos, he regards it as the star that shone above the Child, for which reason he says:

And the star came and stood over where the Child was. Matt 2:9 (DLJC p. 45)

After censing the first veil or cover, he covers the holy bread and diskos with it, reciting the Psalm in which the wonderful majesty of the Lord is sung:

He is clothed with majesty; the Lord is clothed with strength and He hath girt Himself. Ps 93 (DLJC p. 45)

After censing the second veil, he covers the holy chalice with it, saying:

Thy virtue, hath covered the heavens, O Christ, and the earth is full of Thy praise. (DLJC p. 45)

Then the priest takes the large cover, called the holy aer, and covers both chalice and diskos, calling upon God to cover us under the shelter of His wings. And as he steps back from the table of oblation, both he and the deacon bow to the holy bread as the shepherds and kings bowed before the newborn Child, and he censes before the cave as a symbol of the incense, myrrh, and gold that were brought by the Wise Men.

The deacon, as before, attentively follows the priest, and says at every act: **Let us pray to the Lord** (DLJC p. 47), thereby reminding the priest of the beginning of each action. Finally, he takes the censer from the priest and reminds him of the prayer that must be offered to the Lord for these gifts prepared for Him, with the words:

For the precious gifts offered, let us pray to the Lord.
(DLJC p. 47)

Then the priest begins the prayer. Although these gifts have only been prepared for the offering, yet from now on they may not be put to any other use, and the priest reads a prayer in anticipation of the acceptance of these gifts that have been prepared for the coming offering, with these words:

O God, our God, Who didst send forth the Heavenly Bread, the food of the whole world, our Lord and God, Jesus Christ, the Saviour and Redeemer and Benefactor Who blesseth and sanctifieth us: Do Thou Thyself bless this offering, and accept it upon Thy most heavenly altar. As Thou art good and the Lover of mankind, remember those that offer it, and those for whose sake it was offered; and keep us uncondemned in the ministry of Thy Divine Mysteries. (DLJC p. 49)

Directly after this prayer, the priest says the dismissal of the proskomedia, which marks the end of the Office of Oblation.

The deacon censes the offering and then all around the altar in the form of a cross. As he meditates on the earthly birth of Him Who was born before all ages, Who is always present everywhere and universally, he recites to himself:

In the grave bodily, but in Hades with Thy soul as God; in Paradise with the thief, and on the throne with the Father and the Spirit, wast Thou Who fillest all things, O Christ the Inexpressible. (DLJC p. 51)

The deacon goes out of the altar (sanctuary) with the censer in his hand to fill the church with fragrance and to greet all who have gathered at the holy table of love. This censing is always done at the commencement of the service, just as in the home life of all ancient peoples of the East where every guest was offered ablutions and perfumes upon entering the house. This custom was transferred to the heavenly banquet or mystical supper, which bears the name of Liturgy, in which the worship of God is so wonderfully linked with gracious hospitality to all. In this our Saviour Himself gave the example by serving everyone and washing their feet.

Censing and bowing to all, rich and poor, the deacon as God's servant salutes them all as the dearest guests of the heavenly Householder. At the same time, he censes and bows to the icons of the saints, for they too are guests who have come to the mystical supper. In Christ all are alive and inseparable. Having prepared the church by filling it with fragrance, he goes back into the altar and senses the holy table again. Finally, he puts the censer aside and goes to the priest, and both stand before the holy table.

They make three bows to the waist, and as they are preparing to begin the actual celebration of the Liturgy, they invoke the Holy Spirit, for all their service or worship must be spiritual. The Spirit is a teacher and guide in prayer. "For we know do not know what we should pray for as we ought, but the Spirit Himself makes intercession for us with groanings which cannot be uttered" (Romans 8:26), says the Apostle Paul. Praying to the Holy Spirit to dwell in them, and by so doing, to purify them for their service, the priest and deacon repeat the song with which the angels greeted the birth of Jesus Christ:

Glory to God in the highest, and on earth peace, good will among men. Luke 2:14 (DLJC p. 53)

Before this song (when the church is first censed during the reading of the Hours), the altar curtain is drawn back. It is a symbol of those higher spiritual doors that are not opened until we force our thoughts upwards in the contemplation of what is highest. The opening of these higher doors immediately after the song of the angels indicates that the birth of Christ was not revealed to all but known only to the angels in heaven, to Mary and Joseph, to the Wise Men who came to worship Him, and in the distant past to the prophets who foresaw it.

Priest and deacon say softly:

O Lord, Thou shalt open my lips and my mouth shall declare Thy praise. (DLJC p. 53)

The priest kisses the Book of the Gospels, while the deacon kisses the holy table and gives the sign for the Liturgy to begin: holding his orarion with three fingers of his right hand, he says:

It is time to act for the Lord. Bless, Master. (DLJC p. 53)

The priest blesses him with the words:

Blessed is our God, always, now and ever, and to the ages of ages. (DLJC p. 53)

Thinking of the service before him, in which he should be like an angel—by his "flying" from the holy table to the people and from the people to the holy table (and also by gathering all into a single soul and being, so to speak, a holy rousing force)—and feeling his own unworthiness, the deacon humbly says to the priest:

Pray for me, Master. (DLJC p. 53)

The priest replies:

May the Lord direct thy steps. (DLJC p. 53)

The deacon says again:

Remember me, holy master. (DLJC p. 55)

The priest responds.

May the Lord God remember thee in His kingdom, always, now and ever, and to the ages of ages. (DLJC p. 55)

Softly but firmly the deacon says: **Amen** (DLJC p. 55), and goes out of the altar by the north door of the iconostasis[5] to the people and stands on the tribune or ambo in front of the holy doors and again silently repeats:

O Lord, Thou shalt open my lips and my mouth shall declare Thy praise. (DLJC p. 55)

Then he calls to the priest in a loud voice:

Bless, master. (DLJC p. 55)

From the depths of the altar, the priest exclaims:

Blessed is the kingdom of the Father and of the Son and of the Holy Spirit, always, now and ever, and to the ages of ages. (DLJC p. 59)

and the Liturgy proper begins.

The Liturgy of the Catechumens

The second part of the Liturgy is called the Liturgy of the Catechumens, or the Learners. The first part corresponded to the early period of Christ's life: to His birth, revealed only to the angels and to a few persons; and to His childhood and the hidden years of waiting until the time of His public appearance to the world. The second part of the Liturgy corresponds to His life in the world among men, whom He instructed with the word of truth. This part is also called the Liturgy of the Catechumens because in the early days of Christianity even persons who were only preparing to become Christians and who had not yet received holy baptism were admitted to it, although still in the grade of catechumens or learners. Besides, the very form of the office—which consists of readings from the Prophets, from the Apostle and the Holy Gospel—is preeminently catechetical.

The priest begins the Liturgy with the exclamation from inside the altar:

**Blessed is the kingdom of the Father and of the Son and
of the Holy Spirit . . . .** (DLJC p. 59)

Because it was through the incarnation of the Son
that the mystery of the Trinity became clear and evident
to the world, the Trinitarian exclamation precedes and
lights the way for the beginning of each action; and from
the very first moment the worshipper should become
detached from everything and place himself in the realm
of the Trinity.

The deacon, standing on the ambo facing the holy
doors, symbolizes the angel who motivates us to pray. He
raises the orarion, the symbol of the angel's wing, with
three fingers of his right hand and calls the whole assem-
bled congregation to pray the same prayers that have been
used by the Church unchanged since Apostolic times,
beginning with the petition for peace, without which
prayer is impossible. The worshippers make the sign of
the cross, and while striving to make their hearts the har-
moniously tuned strings of an instrument on which each
of the deacon's appeals should strike, they cry mentally
with the choir as it sings:

Lord, have mercy. (DLJC p. 59)

Standing on the ambo, holding the orarion, which
represents the uplifted wing of the angel inciting the people to pray, the deacon calls to prayer: for the peace from
above and the salvation of our souls; for the peace of the

whole world; for the welfare of the holy churches of God and the union of all; for this holy temple and for those who enter it with faith, reverence and the fear of God; for the emperor, the Synod, the ecclesiastical and civil authorities, the palace, the army, and the city; for the monastery or church where the Liturgy is being celebrated; for seasonable weather, for abundance of the fruits of the earth, and for peaceful times; for those travelling by land and water; for the sick and the suffering; for prisoners and captives, and for their salvation; and for our deliverance from all tribulation, fear, danger, and want. And gathering everything in this all-embracing chain of intercession, which is called the Great Litany, at each separate petition the congregation and choir cry:

Lord, have mercy. (DLJC p. 59)

The deacon directs his gaze towards the icons of the Mother of God and the saints depicted on the iconostasis,[1] as a sign of the weakness of our prayers which lack spiritual purity and heavenly direction, and he admonishes the faithful to remember those who are able to pray better than we can and who now intercede for us in heaven. He urges us to entrust ourselves and each other and all our life to Christ our God. With the sincere desire to surrender themselves and each other and their whole life to Christ our God, as did the Mother of God, the saints and those who were better than we are, the whole church cries:

To Thee, O Lord. (DLJC p. 69)

The priest concludes this chain of prayer with a doxology to the Holy Trinity that, like a binding thread through the entire Liturgy, begins and ends its every act. The congregation responds with the affirmative: **Amen** (DLJC p. 70), which means: so be it. The deacon leaves the ambo, and the singing of the antiphons begins. The antiphons are songs selected from the Psalms, which prophetically represent the coming of the Son of God into the world, whose verses are sung responsorially by the two choirs on either side.

During the singing of the first antiphon, the priest prays silently in the altar, while the deacon stands in an attitude of prayer in front of the icon of our Saviour, holding up his orarion with three fingers of his right hand. At the end of this antiphon, the deacon returns to the ambo to call the congregation to prayer with the words:

Again and again, in peace let us pray to the Lord. (DLJC p. 69)

The worshippers respond: **Lord, have mercy** (DLJC p. 69). Looking towards the icons of the saints, the deacon again summons us to remember the Mother of God and all the saints and to entrust ourselves and each other and all our life to Christ our God. The choir answers for all the worshippers: **To Thee, O Lord** (DLJC p. 69). The litany ends with praise to the Trinity, and the whole church responds:

Amen (DLJC p. 71). During the second antiphon, the priest prays silently in the altar. The deacon again stands in an attitude of prayer before the icon of our Redeemer, his orarion held aloft with three fingers of his right hand. When the singing ends, he goes to the ambo and says:

> **Again and again, in peace let us pray to the Lord.** (DLJC p. 73)

The congregation answers: **Lord, have mercy** (DLJC p. 73). The deacon says:

> **Help us, save us, have mercy on us and keep us O God, by Thy grace.** (DLJC p. 73)

The congregation responds: **Lord, have mercy** (DLJC p. 75). The deacon continues:

> **Calling to remembrance our most holy, most pure, most blessed, glorious Lady Theotokos and Ever-Virgin Mary, with all the saints, let us commit ourselves and one another and all our life unto Christ, our God.** (DLJC p. 75)

The congregation responds: **To Thee, O Lord** (DLJC p. 75). The litany ends with praise to the Trinity, and the whole church answers: **Amen** (DLJC p. 75). The deacon leaves the ambo and the priest prays silently in the altar the following prayer:

> **O Thou Who hast bestowed upon us these common and concordant prayers, and Who hast promised that when two or three are agreed in Thy name Thou wouldst grant their requests: Do Thou Thyself fulfill the requests of Thy servants to their profit, granting us in this present age the knowledge of Thy truth, and in that to come, life everlasting.** (DLJC p. 75)

The Beatitudes proclaimed by the Gospel of Christ loudly resound from the choir for all to hear.

The congregation, with the cry of the penitent thief who called to Christ on the cross: **In Thy kingdom remember us, O Lord, when Thou comest in Thy kingdom** (DLJC p. 77), repeats after the reader the words of our Saviour:

> **Blessed are the poor in spirit for theirs is the kingdom of heaven;** (DLJC p. 77)

which means blessed are the humble who are not puffed up in their minds.

> **Blessed are they that mourn, for they shall be comforted;** (DLJC p. 77)

that is, blessed are those who weep and are troubled more over their own imperfections and sins than over the slights and insults they receive from others.

Blessed are the meek, for they shall inherit the earth; (DLJC p. 77)

which means blessed are those who do not harbor anger towards anyone, but who forgive and love, and whose weapon is invincible gentleness.

Blessed are those who hunger and thirst for righteousness, for they shall be filled; (DLJC p. 77)

that is, blessed are those who hunger for heavenly righteousness, truth, and justice, and who thirst to restore it first in themselves.

Blessed are the merciful, for they shall obtain mercy; (DLJC p. 77)

which means blessed are those who have compassion or sympathy for every brother, and who see in every suppliant Christ Himself.

Blessed are the pure in heart, for they shall see God; (DLJC p. 77)

that is, just as in the clean mirror of still water, untroubled by sand or mud, the vault of heaven is clearly reflected, so in the mirror of a pure heart, untroubled by passions, nothing human is reflected, except the image of God.

Blessed are the peacemakers, for they shall be called sons of God; (DLJC p. 77) which means blessed are those who, like the Son of God Who came to earth to bring peace to our souls, bring peace and reconciliation into homes as true sons of God.

> **Blessed are they that are persecuted for righteousness' sake, for theirs is the kingdom of heaven;** (DLJC p. 77)

that is, blessed are those who are persecuted for their preaching and defense of justice and righteousness, not only in words but also by the fragrance of their whole life.

> **Blessed are ye when men shall revile and persecute you and say all manner of evil against you falsely for My sake. Rejoice and be exceeding glad, for your reward is great in the Heavens;** (DLJC p. 77)

great are they, for their merit is threefold: first, because they were innocent and pure; second, because although they were pure, they were slandered; and third, because although they were slandered, they rejoiced that they were suffering for Christ.

The congregation tearfully repeats these words of our Saviour that proclaim who can expect and hope for eternal life in the world to come and who will be the true heirs and partakers of the kingdom of Heaven.

At this point, the holy doors are solemnly opened, as though they were the gates of heaven itself, and before the eyes of the whole congregation stands the resplendent altar as the dwelling of God's glory and the place of spiritual instruction from which the knowledge of the truth goes out to us and eternal life is proclaimed. The priest and deacon go to the holy table and take the Book of the Gospels from it, which they carry to the people, not by way of the holy doors but through a side-door, reminiscent of the door in that side room from which in early times the books were carried out to the middle of the church to be read.

The faithful look upon the Gospel, which is carried in the hands of the humble ministers of the Church, as if it were the Saviour Himself going out for the first time to do the work of divine preaching. He goes out through the narrow north door, as if unrecognized, into the middle of the temple, so that when He has shown Himself to everyone He may return to the altar through the holy doors. God's ministers stop in the center of the church (before the iconostasis). Both bow their heads. The priest prays secretly, so that He Who established the armies of angels in heaven and the heavenly ranks to minister to His glory may now order these same celestial powers and angels who serve with us to make the entry with us into the altar. The deacon, pointing with the orarion towards the holy doors, says:

Bless, master, the holy entrance. (DLJC p. 81)

Blessed is the entry of Thy saints, always, now and ever, and unto the ages of ages, (DLJC p. 81) exclaims the priest. After giving him the Holy Gospel to kiss, the deacon carries it into the altar, but stops in the holy doors and, raising it in his hands, exclaims: **Wisdom** (DLJC p. 81), indicating by this the wisdom proclaimed to the world through the Gospel. Then he says: **Stand aright** (DLJC p. 81), whereby he exhorts the worshippers to stand with reverence. Uplifted in spirit, they sing with the choir:

> **O come, let us worship and fall down before Christ; O Son of God, Who art wondrous in the saints (on Sundays: Who didst rise from the dead), save us who chant unto Thee. Alleluia.** (DLJC p. 81)

In Hebrew the word **Alleluia** means "The Lord comes. Praise the Lord!" But because in the holy language the word "comes" contains mystically both the present and the future (i.e., "He who comes and He who will come again"), it symbolizes the eternal coming of God. This word accompanies such holy acts that indicate the Lord Himself going out to the people in the form of the Gospel or the Holy Gifts.

The Gospel, which proclaims the word of life, is placed on the holy table. The choirs sing hymns in honor of the feast of the day or the troparia and hymns in honor of the saint whose day the Church is celebrating, for the saint has become like those whom Christ mentions in the Beatitudes and because he has shown by the living example of his own life how we can rise with Christ to eternal life.

After the troparia comes the time of the Trisagion (the "Holy, Holy, Holy"). The deacon, having asked the priest's blessing, stands in the holy doors and raises his orarion to give the sign to the singers. The Trisagion hymn, which consists of a threefold invocation to God:

Holy God, Holy Mighty, Holy Immortal, have mercy on us,

is sung by the whole church. Thrice the choir sings this song, that it may resound in the ears of all. The priest in the altar prays the silent prayer for the acceptance of this singing of the Trisagion. Thrice he bows before the holy table and thrice he repeats:

Holy God, Holy Mighty, Holy Immortal, have mercy on us.

The deacon also says the Trisagion thrice with the priest and bows thrice before the holy table.

Having performed this threefold act of adoration, the priest goes to the high place, as if into the depths of the knowledge of God, whence the mystery of the Holy Trinity flows out to us, saying:

Blessed is He that cometh in the name of the Lord. (DLJC p. 87)

With trembling steps, the priest goes to the high place, and when the deacon says:

Bless, master, the High Throne, (DLJC p. 87)

the priest replies:

> **Blessed art Thou on the glorious throne of the glory of Thy kingdom, Thou that sittest on the Cherubim, always, now and ever, and to the ages of ages.** (DLJC p. 87)

The priest sits while the Apostle is being read—not in the high place, which is reserved for the bishop, but to the side of it. From there, as God's Apostle, with his face turned towards the people, he prepares them to listen attentively to the reading of the Apostolic epistle. The reader goes with the Book of the Apostle to the middle of the church, and the deacon calls all present to listen attentively, saying: **Let us attend** (DLJC p. 87).

The priest sends a wish for peace from the depths of the altar both to the reader and to those present. The congregation responds with the same wish for the priest. But as his ministry should be spiritual, like the ministry of the Apostles who did not speak their own words but whose lips were moved by the Holy Spirit, they do not say to the priest: **Peace be unto all** (DLJC p. 89), but: **And to thy spirit** (DLJC p. 89). The deacon exclaims: **Wisdom** (DLJC p. 89). Loudly and distinctly the reader begins so that every word may be heard by everyone. The congregation attends diligently with receptive hearts and seeking souls, their minds searching for the inner meaning of what is read. For the reading of the Apostle serves as a kind of series of steps or ladder to the subsequent reading of the Gospel. When the reader finishes, the priest calls to him from the altar: **Peace be unto thee** (DLJC p. 89). The reader answers: **And to thy spirit** (DLJC p. 89). Again the deacon exclaims: **Wisdom** (DLJC p. 89). The choir sings: **Alleluia** (DLJC p. 89), which announces the approach of the Lord Who is coming to speak to the people by the words of the Gospel.

Before reading the Gospel, the deacon comes with the censer in his hand to fill the church with sweet fragrance for the reception of the Lord, reminding us by this censing of the spiritual purification of our souls with which we should attend to the fragrant words of the Gospel. The priest in the altar prays silently that the light of the knowledge of God may shine in our hearts and that the eyes of our minds may be opened to the understanding of the Gospel message. The faithful also pray inwardly for the shining of this light in their hearts as they prepare to listen. After asking the priest's blessing and receiving reassurance from him:

> **May God, through the prayers of the holy, glorious, all-praised Apostle and Evangelist [name] give speech with great power unto thee that bringest good tidings, unto the fulfillment of the Gospel of His beloved Son, our Lord Jesus Christ,** (DLJC p. 93)

the deacon goes to the ambo preceded by a man carrying a candle. This signifies the all-illuminating Light of

Christ, which was preceded by the lamp of the Light, the Lord's Forerunner. The priest in the altar exclaims to the congregation:

Wisdom. Aright! Let us hear the Holy Gospel. Peace unto all. (DLJC p. 93)

The choir answers: **And to thy spirit** (DLJC p. 93), and the deacon begins to read.

Reverently bowing their heads and attending to the reading of the Gospel from the ambo, as though listening to Christ Himself speaking as He spoke the Beatitudes on the mountain, all try to receive with their hearts the seed of the sacred word, which the Heavenly Sower sows by the mouth of His minister. Not with hearts that the Saviour compares to the wayside on which the seeds fall but are stolen by birds—that is, by evil thoughts that swoop down on them. Not with hearts that He compares to rocky ground covered with a thin layer of soil on the top and which gladly receive the word, yet it does not take deep root because depth of heart is lacking. Nor with hearts that He compares to untilled land overgrown with thorns, in which the seed comes up but is soon choked by the thorns which grow up with it—that is, worldly cares and troubles and the countless lures and attractions of a worldly, moribund life, a life of deceptive comforts that stifle the sprouts that have scarcely appeared, so that the seed remains without fruit. But they try to receive God's word with those receptive hearts that He compares to good ground that bears fruit, some thirty, some sixty, and some a hundredfold. And after leaving church, they cultivate all that they have received—at home, in the family, in service, at work and at leisure, in conversation and in solitude. Every believer strives to be at once both listener and doer, whom the Saviour compares to a wise man who built his house not on sand but on rock, so that even if the rains and floods and storms of hardships were to fall upon him just after leaving church, his spiritual house would remain unmoved like a fortress on a rock.

After the reading is finished, the priest from the altar exclaims to the deacon:

Peace be unto thee that bringest Good Tidings. (DLJC p. 95)

Having been granted to hear the Holy Gospel, all present with a sense of gratitude sing with the choir:

Glory to Thee, O Lord, glory to Thee. (DLJC p. 95)

Standing in the holy doors, the priest receives the Book of the Gospels from the deacon and places it on the holy table as the Word coming from God and returning to Him. The altar which represents the abode on high, is now hidden from view. The holy doors are closed, indicating that there are no other doors into the kingdom of heaven except the one that was opened by Jesus Christ when He said: **I am the Door (John 10:9).**

At this point, it was usual in the early days of Christianity to have a sermon explaining or interpreting the Gospel lesson. Nowadays, as the sermon is frequently based on other texts and not on the Gospel of the day, it is left to the end in order not to disrupt the continuity of the Liturgy.

Symbolizing the angel who exhorts people to pray, the deacon goes to the ambo to urge the congregation to pray still more vigorously and fervently:

Let us all say with all our whole soul and with our whole mind let us say: (DLJC p. 95)

calls out the deacon, with his orarion raised with three fingers. Those present respond: **Lord, have mercy** (DLJC p. 95). Intensifying the prayers by a threefold cry for mercy, the deacon again calls for prayers by all persons of different professions and ranks, commencing with the highest for whom the difficulties are greatest, for whom there are more obstacles and who have the greatest need of God's help. Each of the congregation, knowing how much the welfare of the people depends on the governing authorities carrying out their duties honestly, prays for them with special zeal, saying not once, but thrice: **Lord, have mercy** (DLJC p. 93). The whole chain of these petitions is called the Augmented Litany or the Litany of Fervent Supplication. The priest prays in the altar before the holy table for its acceptance his own prayer called the Prayer of Fervent Supplication.

If prayers for the departed are to be offered, they are read now. Holding his orarion in his right hand, the deacon calls the congregation to pray for the repose of the souls of God's servants, whom he mentions by name, asking God's forgiveness for their voluntary and involuntary transgressions, so that He will establish their souls where the righteous repose. Here everyone present remembers the departed who are nearest and dearest to his heart and says silently after every petition of the deacon: **Lord, have mercy**, and prays both for his own family and friends and for all departed Christians:

The mercy of God, the kingdom of heaven, and the remission of their sins, let us ask of Christ the immortal King and our God. (DLJC p. 103)

The worshippers and the choir sing: **Grant this, O Lord** (DLJC p. 103). The priest, however, prays in the altar that He Who has overcome death and has given us life may lead the souls of His departed servants to a place of light, of joy, and of refreshment, whence pain, sorrow, and sighing flee, and after praying for the remission of their sins, he says aloud:

For Thou art the resurrection and the life and the repose of Thy departed servants, O Christ our God, and unto Thee do we send up glory, together with Thy unoriginate Father, and Thy Most-holy and good and life-creating Spirit, now and ever, and to the ages of ages. (DLJC p. 105)

The choir answers: **Amen** (DLJC p. 105). The deacon begins the Litany of the Catechumens.

Although in our days it is rare to find people who have not received baptism and are numbered among the catechumens, nevertheless everyone present, thinking how far he is from those believers in the early days of Christianity who were granted to be present at the table of love, counts himself a learner or catechumen. He sees, we may say, that he is instructed by Christ but knows that he has not yet admitted Him into his own life; he knows that he hears the meaning of Christ's words but does not realize them in his own life and that his faith is still cold and the flame of all-forgiving love towards his fellows is wanting, this flame which melts callousness of soul. Weighing all this, he stands contritely in the ranks of the learners. At the deacon's exclamation: **Pray, ye catechumens, to the Lord** (DLJC p. 105), he calls out from the depths of his contrite heart: **Lord, have mercy** (DLJC p. 105). The deacon says:

> **Ye faithful, let us pray for the catechumens that the Lord will have mercy on them. That He will catechize them with the word of truth. That He will reveal unto them the Gospel of righteousness. That He will unite them to His Holy, Catholic and Apostolic Church. Save them, have mercy on them, help them, and keep them, O God, by Thy grace.** (DLJC pp. 105–107)

The faithful, realizing how unworthy they are to be addressed as believers, pray for the catechumens, for themselves and after every petition of the deacon, they say in contrition of heart after the singers: **Lord, have mercy** (DLJC pp. 105–107). The deacon says: **Ye catechumens, bow your heads unto the Lord** (DLJC p. 107).

All present bow their heads and sing from their hearts: **To Thee, O Lord** (DLJC p. 107). The priest prays silently for the learners and for those who in humility of soul have placed themselves among the learners. His prayer reads:

> **O Lord our God, Who dwellest on high and lookest down on things that are lowly, Who unto the human race hast sent forth salvation, Thine Only-begotten Son and God, our Lord Jesus Christ: look upon Thy servants, the catechumens, who have bowed their necks before Thee, and vouchsafe unto them at a seasonable time the laver of regeneration, the remission of sins, and the garment of incorruption; unite them to Thy Holy, Catholic, and Apostolic Church, and number them among Thy chosen flock.** (DLJC p. 107)

Then he adds, aloud:

> **That they also with us may glorify Thine most honorable and majestic name: of the Father, and of the Son, and of the Holy Spirit, now and ever, and to the ages of ages.**
> (DLJC p. 109)

The choir sings: **Amen.** As a reminder that the moment has come when the catechumens formerly were led out of the church, the deacon says:

As many as are catechumens, depart. Catechumens, depart. Let none of the catechumens remain. As many as are of the faithful: again and again, in peace pray to the Lord. (DLJC p. 109)

At these words all present shudder, all who feel their unworthiness. Calling mentally upon Christ Himself Who drove out of the temple of God the disorderly vendors and shameless traders who had turned His altar into a market, every person tries to drive out of the temple of his own soul the carnal man, the catechumen who is not ready to be present at the sacred action. Everyone calls upon Christ Himself that He may raise up in him the hidden man of the heart, the man of faith, numbered among the chosen flock, of whom the Apostle said: "A holy nation, new men, living stones built into a spiritual temple." (Cf. 1 Pet 2:5,9; also Eph 4:24.) Each person prays that he may be numbered among the true believers who were present at the Liturgy in the first centuries of Christianity, whose faces look down at him from the iconostasis. Embracing them all at a glance, the worshipper calls upon them for help, as brothers now praying in heaven, that by their prayers they may raise up in him the true believer, for the most sacred acts are about to take place. The Liturgy of the Faithful begins.

The Liturgy of the Faithful

In the closed altar, the priest unfolds on the holy table the antimension (which means "in place of a table"), a cloth with a picture of the burial of our Saviour. The antimension contains holy relics and on it must be placed the holy bread and the chalice containing wine mixed with water which are prepared by the priest during the proskomedia, and which will now be solemnly transferred from the Table of Oblation in the sight of all the faithful.

The antimension recalls the times of the persecution of the Christians when the Church had no permanent abode and could not carry a table from place to place. The use of this cloth with portions of relics began at that time, and it has been retained as a reminder that the Church of Christ is not confined to any particular building, city, or place, but is like a ship borne on the waves of this world and casting her anchor nowhere—her anchor is in heaven.

After unfolding the antimension, the priest stands before the holy table as though he were approaching it for the first time and is only now preparing to begin the real service. For in the early times of Christianity the altar remained closed and curtained until this point, and it was only now opened and the real prayers of the faithful began.

Still within the closed altar, the priest falls down before the holy table and in the two prayers of the faithful prays for his purification and that he may be made worthy to stand before the holy table without condemnation and offer sacrifices with the pure witness of his conscience.

The deacon, standing on the ambo in the midst of the church and holding his orarion with three fingers, calls all the faithful to the same prayers with which the Liturgy of the Catechumens began.

Striving to bring their hearts into the harmonious unity of peace, which is now more imperative than ever, all the faithful cry: **Lord, have mercy** (DLJC p. 113), and still more fervently pray for the peace from above and for the salvation of their souls, for the peace of the whole world, for the welfare of the holy Churches of God and the union of all, for the holy temple and for those who enter it with faith, reverence, and fear of God, and for deliverance from all tribulation, danger, and want. And in their hearts they cry with still greater vigor: **Lord, have mercy** (DLJC p. 113).

The deacon exclaims: **Wisdom**, to indicate that the same Wisdom, the same Eternal Son of God Who came out in the form of the Book of the Gospels to sow the word of life, is now to be brought forth in the form of the holy bread as a sacrifice for all the world. Startled by this reminder, all the worshippers direct their thoughts to the holy acts about to begin. Meanwhile, the priest at the holy table prays this sublime prayer:

None is worthy among them that are bound with carnal lusts and pleasures, to approach or to draw nigh, or to minister unto Thee, O King of glory, for to serve Thee is a great and fearful thing even unto the heavenly hosts themselves. Yet because of Thine ineffable and immeasurable love for mankind, without change or alteration Thou didst become man, and didst become our High Priest, and didst deliver unto us the ministry of this liturgical and bloodless sacrifice for Thou art the Master of all. Thou alone, O Lord our God, dost rule over those in heaven and those on earth, art borne upon the throne of the Cherubim, art Lord of the Seraphim and King of Israel, Thou alone art holy and restest in the saints. I implore Thee, therefore, Who alone art good and inclined to listen: Look upon me, Thy sinful and unprofitable servant, and purge my soul and heart of a wicked conscience, and by the power of Thy Holy Spirit, enable me, who am clothed with the grace of the priesthood, to stand before this Thy Holy Table, and to perform the sacred Mystery of Thy holy and immaculate Body and precious Blood. For unto Thee do I draw nigh, bowing my neck, and I pray Thee: Turn not Thy countenance away from me, neither cast me out from among Thy children, but

vouchsafe that these gifts be offered unto Thee by me, Thy sinful and unworthy servant: for Thou art He that offereth and is offered, that accepteth and is distributed, O Christ our God, and unto Thee do we send up glory, together with Thine unoriginate Father, and Thy Most-holy and good and life-creating Spirit, now and ever, and unto the ages of ages. (DLJC pp. 117–119)

Before this prayer, the holy doors are opened and the priest is seen praying with uplifted hands. The deacon with the censer in his hand comes out to prepare the way for the King of All and by the abundantly dispersed incense rising in clouds of fragrance through which the Holy Gifts are carried, he reminds all that their prayer should be directed like incense before the Lord so that all who, in the words of the Apostle, are a fragrance for Christ should keep in mind that they are to be pure as Cherubim in order to receive the Lord. The choirs on either side sing in the name of the whole Church the so-called Cherubic Hymn:

Let us who mystically represent the Cherubim and chant the thrice-holy hymn unto the life-creating Trinity, now lay aside all earthly care. That we may receive the King of all, Who cometh invisibly upborne in triumph by the ranks of angels. Alleluia alleluia, alleluia. (DLJC p. 119)

This **Alleluia** is called the Cherubic Hymn because according to Holy Scripture the Cherubim praise the Lord with this exclamation.

To understand this hymn, one must know that among the ancient Romans it was the custom to carry out the newly elected emperor to the people surrounded by his legions on a shield raised aloft on spears and canopied by a forest of inclined spears and standards held above him, amid loud cries of: "Long live the emperor!" And one must know, moreover, that this song was composed by one of the ancient emperors who humbled himself to the dust with all his earthly majesty before the Majesty of the King of All Who is borne as on spears by Cherubim and legions of the heavenly hosts.

Meanwhile, the priest and deacon, having recited silently the same Cherubic Hymn, go to the Table of Oblation at the side where the proskomedia was performed. The deacon goes to the Holy Gifts covered with the aer and says to the priest: **Lift up, master** (DLJC p. 121). The priest takes the aer, places it on the deacon's left shoulder and says:

Lift up your hands to the holy place and bless the Lord.
(DLJC p. 121)

Then he takes the diskos with the "Lamb" and places it on the deacon's head, while he himself takes the holy chalice. Then preceded by a lamp or candle, they go out through the north door to the people. If the service is being celebrated by several priests, one carries the chalice, another the holy cross, a third the communion spoon, and a fourth the spear. In brief, almost all the vessels of the holy sacrifice are taken out, even the sponge with which the crumbs of holy bread are collected on the diskos, which represents the sponge steeped in vinegar and gall with which men quenched their Creator's thirst.

The choir, which has sung the first part of the Cherubim Hymn, is silent for a time. And just then, resembling the heavenly hosts, this solemn procession of clergy comes out, known as the Great Entrance. At the sight of the King of All carried in the humble form of the "Lamb" lying on the diskos (as on a shield) and surrounded by the instruments of His earthly Passion like the spears of countless heavenly hosts and orders, all present bow their heads and pray in the words of the thief on the cross:

Lord, remember me when Thou comest into Thy kingdom. Luke 23:42

In the midst of the temple, the whole procession stops. The Church uses this great moment to remember before God the names of all Christians, beginning with those on whom the most difficult and most sacred duties have been laid and on the carrying out of which depends the happiness of all and the salvation of their own souls. This prayer concludes with the words:

And all of you Orthodox Christians, may the Lord God remember in His kingdom, always, now and ever, and to the ages of ages. (DLJC p. 123)

The singers conclude their moving song:

> **That we may receive the King of all, Who cometh invisibly upborne in triumph by the ranks of angels.** (DLJC p. 119)

with the threefold cry of the Cherubim: **Alleluia,** which announces and accompanies this mystical procession of the King of kings and Lord of lords as He goes to His voluntary suffering and death for the salvation of the world. The procession goes through the holy doors. First the deacon enters the altar and stops on the right side of the doors. He receives the priest with the words:

> **May the Lord God remember thy priesthood in His kingdom.** (DLJC p. 125)

The priest responds:

> **May the Lord God remember thy sacred diaconate in His kingdom, always, now and ever, and to the ages of ages.** (DLJC p. 125)

The priest places the holy chalice and the bread representing the form of the Body of Christ on the holy table as if in the grave. The holy doors are closed as if they were the doors of the Lord's tomb; the curtain is drawn as if it were the guard stationed before the Sepulcher. The priest takes the holy diskos from the deacon's head as if he were

taking the Body of our Saviour Himself from the cross
and places it on the unfolded antimension as on a shroud,
accompanying this action with the words:

> **The noble Joseph, having taken Thy most pure body
> down from the Tree and wrapped It in pure linen and
> covered It with spices, laid It in a new tomb.** (DLJC
> p. 125)

And remembering the omnipresence of Him Who now
lies before him in the grave, the priest says to himself:

> **In the grave bodily, but in Hades with Thy soul as God;
> in Paradise with the thief; and on the throne with the
> Father and the Spirit wast Thou Who fillest all things, O
> Christ the Inexpressible.** (DLJC p. 125)

And remembering the glory with which the Grave was
filled, he says:

> **How life-giving, how much more beautiful than Paradise
> and truly more resplendent than any royal palace hath Thy
> tomb appeared, O Christ, the source of our resurrection.**
> (DLJC p. 125)

After taking the veils or covers from the diskos and chalice, and taking the aer from the deacon's shoulder—now
no longer representing the swaddles in which the Child
Jesus was wrapped, but rather the shroud and grave-cloths

in which His dead Body was wrapped—the priest again covers the diskos and chalice with the aer, saying:

> **The noble Joseph, having taken Thy most pure Body down from the Tree....** (DLJC p. 125)

Then the deacon gives him the censer and he censes the Holy Gifts and says to himself the words of the Prophet David in preparation for the coming sacrifice:

> **Do good, O Lord, in Thy good pleasure unto Sion, and let the walls of Jerusalem be builded. Then shalt Thou be pleased with a sacrifice of righteousness, with oblation and whole-burnt offerings. Than shall they offer bullocks upon Thine altar.** (DLJC p. 127)

For unless God Himself builds and protects our souls with the walls of Jerusalem from all temptations of the flesh, we are incapable of offering Him sacrifices or offerings, and the flame of spiritual prayer cannot rise on high but is blown about by irrelevant thoughts, by outbursts of the passions and a storm of mental unrest. Praying for his purification for the coming sacrifice, the priest gives the censer back to the deacon and with bowed head says to him:

> **Pray for me, brother and concelebrant.** (DLJC p. 127)

The deacon replies:

> **The Holy Spirit shall come upon thee, and the power of the Most High shall overshadow thee.** (DLJC p. 127)

Then in his turn, thinking of his own unworthiness, the deacon bows his head and holding the orarion in his hand, he says:

Remember me, holy master. (DLJC p. 127)

The priest answers:

May the Lord God remember thee in His kingdom, always, now and ever, and unto the ages of ages. (DLJC p. 127)

The deacon says: **Amen** (DLJC p. 127), kisses his hand and goes through the north door to call upon all present to pray for the Holy Gifts that have been transferred to the altar.

Going to the ambo, facing the holy doors and holding up the orarion with three fingers of his right hand, like the outspread wings of an angel urging us to pray, the deacon offers a chain of petitions, unlike those previously read. Beginning with a call to pray for the Gifts that have been transferred to the holy table, he continues to those petitions which only the faithful living in Christ can offer to the Lord. The deacon exclaims:

That the whole day may be perfect, holy, peaceful and sinless, let us ask of the Lord. (DLJC p. 131)

And praying for such a day, in union with the choir of singers, the people present cry from their hearts:

Grant this, O Lord.
An angel of peace, a faithful guide, a guardian of our souls and bodies, let us ask of the Lord. (DLJC p. 131)

And praying for the angel, all cry:

Grant this, O Lord.
Pardon and remission of our sins and offenses, let us ask of the Lord. (DLJC p. 131)

Imploring forgiveness with tears, all cry:

Grant this, O Lord.
Things good and profitable for our souls, and peace for the world, let us ask of the Lord. (DLJC p. 131)

And praying for everything good and profitable for their souls and for what is most essential for the world, the worshippers cry more vigorously:

Grant this, O Lord.
That we may complete the remaining time of our life in peace and repentance, let us ask of the Lord. (DLJC p. 133)

Praying for this as for what is most to be desired for a Christian, the congregation cries:

Grant this, O Lord.
A Christian ending to our life, painless, blameless, peaceful, and a good defense at the dread judgment seat of Christ, let us ask of the Lord. (DLJC p. 133)

Uniting in one shout the prayer of the whole congregation, all cry:

Grant this, O Lord. (DLJC p. 133)

Lifting up his bodily and spiritual eyes towards the icons or figures of the saints, the deacon exclaims:

Calling to remembrance our most holy, most pure, most blessed, glorious Lady Theotokos and Ever-Virgin Mary, with all the Saints, let us commit ourselves and one another, and all our life to Christ, our God. (DLJC p. 133)

With a true desire, like the Mother of God and the saints, to surrender themselves and one another to Christ, all cry:

To Thee, O Lord. (DLJC p. 133)

The litany concludes with the exclamation:

Through the compassions of Thine only-begotten Son, with Whom Thou art blessed, together with Thine all-holy and good and life-creating Spirit, now and ever, and to the ages of ages. (DLJC p. 133)

The choir sings: **Amen** (DLJC p. 133).

The altar is still closed. The priest has not yet begun to offer the sacrifice. There is much to be done beforehand.

The priest prepares to commemorate the mystical supper. The altar now becomes the upper room where it took place. The holy table is the table. The whole temple of worshippers must now be changed into the group of disciples who were present at the Last Supper. From the depths of the altar the priest greets the faithful with the Saviour's own greeting: **Peace to all** (DLJC p. 135). They respond:

And with thy spirit. (DLJC p. 135)

Standing on the ambo, as in early Christian times, the deacon calls all to mutual love with the words:

Let us love one another, that with one mind we may confess. (DLJC p. 135)

The choir continues and concludes the deacon's exclamation with the words:

The Father, and the Son and the Holy Spirit: the Trinity, one in essence and indivisible. (DLJC p. 135)

For if we do not love one another, it is impossible to love Him Who is all pure love, complete and perfect. The priest in the altar bows thrice and says silently:

I will love Thee, O Lord, my strength; the Lord is my foundation and my refuge. (DLJC p. 135)

He then kisses the holy diskos covered with the aer, the holy chalice, and the edge of the holy table. However many priests may be concelebrating with him, they all do the same and then kiss one another's hands. The senior priest says:

Christ is in our midst. (DLJC p. 135)

They answer:

He is, and shall be. (DLJC p. 135)

Also the deacons, however many there may be, first kiss their own orarions where the cross is, then each other on the shoulder, and repeat the same words as the priests.

In former times, all present in the church kissed one another, men other men, women other women, saying:

Christ is in our midst,

and others replying:

He is and shall be.

For that reason, even now every person present gathers mentally before him all Christians—not only those present in the church but also those who are absent, not only those who are close to his heart but even those far from his heart, and hastening to be reconciled with all towards whom he has harbored hatred, dislike, or displeasure, he gives them a spiritual kiss, saying inwardly:

Christ is in our midst,

and answering for them:

He is and shall be.

For, without this, he will be dead to all the sacred acts that follow, according to Christ's words:

Leave your gift before the altar and go away. First be reconciled with your brother and then come and offer your gift. Matt 5:24

And according to the saying of Christ's Apostle:

If anyone says: "I love God," and yet hates his brother, he is a liar. For whoever does not love his brother whom he has seen, how can he love God Whom he has not seen? 1 John 4:20

Standing on the ambo and holding the orarion with three fingers, the deacon gives the warning exclamation to those present:

The doors, the doors! (DLJC p. 135)

Formerly this exclamation was addressed to the doorkeepers who stood at the entrance so that no one might be allowed to enter the church who did not have the right to attend the Liturgy of the Faithful. Now this exclamation is addressed to those present, that they may guard the doors of their hearts, where love belongs according to the Church's teaching, so that the spirit of enmity may not invade this inner altar of the soul. But the doors of their lips and ears should be open to hear the Confession of Faith, in token of which the curtain behind the holy doors is drawn back. The curtain represents the doors on high that are opened only when the attention of the mind is directed to the highest mysteries. The deacon calls us to listen to the Confession of Faith with the words:

In wisdom let us attend. (DLJC p. 135)

In firm, strong tones, more like speaking, the singers sing loudly and clearly:

**I believe in one God, the Father Almighty,
Maker of heaven and earth and of all things
visible and invisible; and in one Lord Jesus
Christ, the Son of God, the Only-begotten,
begotten of the Father before all ages, Light
of Light, true God of true God, begotten,
not made, of one essence with the Father,
by Whom all things were made; Who for us
men and for our salvation came down from
the heavens, and was incarnate of the Holy
Spirit and the Virgin Mary, and became man;**

and was crucified for us under Pontius Pilate,
and suffered, and was buried; and arose on
the third day according to the Scriptures; and
ascended into the heavens, and sitteth at the
right hand of the Father; and shall come again,
with glory, to judge both the living and the
dead, Whose kingdom shall have no end. And
in the Holy Spirit, the Lord, the Giver of Life,
Who proceedeth from the Father, Who with
the Father and the Son together is worshipped
and glorified, Who spake by the prophets. In
one Holy, Catholic, and Apostolic Church. I
confess one baptism for the remission of sins.
I look for the resurrection of the dead; and the
life of the age to come. Amen. (DLJC pp. 137–139)

In firm, strong tones that impress every word of this confession on the heart, the singers chant this creed and everyone firmly repeats the words after them. Taking courage in heart and spirit, the priest stands before the holy table, which represents the holy table of the Mystical Supper, and repeats the creed to himself as do all who are serving with him, while waving the holy aer over the Holy Gifts.

With firm step the deacon comes out and exclaims:

Let us stand well. Let us stand with fear. Let us attend, that we may offer the holy oblation in peace. (DLJC p. 139)

That is, let us stand as man ought to stand before God, with fear and trembling and at the same time with bold confidence of spirit, praising God with the restored harmony of peace in our hearts, without which it is impossible to ascend to God. In response to this appeal, all the church, offering as a sacrifice the praise of their lips and the grace in their hearts, repeats after the choir:

A mercy of peace, a sacrifice of praise. (DLJC p. 139)

Meanwhile the priest takes the aer off the Holy Gifts, kisses it, and lays it aside. The deacon goes into the altar and takes the fan, or ripidion, and reverently fans above the Gifts. Preparing for the culmination of the mystery of the Communion, the priest gives the Apostolic greeting to the people from the altar:

The grace of our Lord Jesus Christ, and the love of God the Father, and the communion of the Holy Spirit be with you all. (DLJC p. 139)

All respond:

And with thy spirit. (DLJC p. 141)

The altar, which previously was the crib or cave in which Christ was born, is now the upper room in which the Last Supper was prepared. The holy table, which represented the Tomb, is now the Table, and not the Grave. The priest exclaims:

Let us lift up our hearts. (DLJC p. 141)

And all people standing in the temple think of what is about to be accomplished; namely, that at this moment the Lamb of God comes to be slain for them, that the divine Blood is about to be poured into the chalice for their purification, and all the heavenly powers unite with the priest to pray for them. Thinking of all this and striving to raise their hearts from earth to heaven, from darkness to light, each one cries with all the others:

We lift them up unto the Lord. (DLJC p. 141)

Remembering our Saviour Who gave thanks to God the Father before breaking bread at the Mystical Supper, the priest exclaims:

Let us give thanks to the Lord. (DLJC p. 141)

The choir responds:

It is meet and right to worship the Father, the Son and the Holy Spirit, the Trinity, one in essence and indivisible. (DLJC p. 141)

The priest prays silently:

It is meet and right to hymn Thee, to bless Thee, to praise Thee, to give thanks unto Thee, to worship Thee in every place of Thy dominion, for Thou art God inexpressible,

incomprehensible, invisible, unattainable, ever-existing, eternally the same, Thou and Thine Only-begotten Son and Thy Holy Spirit. Thou didst call us from nonbeing into being, and when we had fallen away, Thou didst raise us up again, and didst not cease to do all things until Thou hadst brought us up to heaven, and hadst bestowed upon us Thy kingdom which is to come. For all these things we give thanks unto Thee, to Thine Only-begotten Son, and to Thy Holy Spirit, for all the things we know, and whereof we know not; for the benefits both manifest and hidden which have come upon us. We give thanks unto Thee also for this service which Thou hast been pleased to accept from our hands, though there stand before Thee thousands of archangels and ten thousands of angels, the cherubim and seraphim, six-winged, many-eyed, borne aloft on their wings. (DLJC pp. 141–143)

Then he prays aloud:

Singing the triumphal hymn, shouting, crying aloud and saying: (DLJC p. 143)

The choir continues:

Holy, holy, holy, Lord of Sabbaoth, heaven and earth are full of Thy glory. (DLJC p. 143)

The three words **Holy, Holy, Holy** (DLJC p. 143) point to the Trinity of the Godhead, while the single phrase **Lord of Sabbaoth** (DLJC p. 143) points to His unity.

To the Hymn of the Seraphim, which resounds in heaven, the Church has added the song with which the Hebrew children met the King of heaven on earth when He made His entry into Jerusalem to offer Himself as a sacrifice:

Hosanna in the highest. Blessed is He that cometh in the Name of the Lord. (DLJC p. 143)

With this song, the whole Church now meets Him as He invisibly comes from heaven into the temple as into the mystical Jerusalem to offer Himself as a sacrifice in the Mystery about to take place. For that reason, just as previously when representing the Cherubim and in union with the heavenly hosts who proclaimed the Incarnation of Christ, everyone present sang the song of the Cherubim to Him Who was borne in triumph by the angelic orders as the King of All, so in union with the flaming Seraphim let everyone now sing to Him the triumphant song of the Seraphim.

"Everyone of you can ascend the heights of the Seraphim, if only you want to do so," says St John Chrysostom. "Only recall and gather in your memory all the most beautiful things that you have seen on earth and which have delighted you, and reflect that all these thing are so lovely only because they are a reflection of the great heavenly beauty, only the gleaming hem of the mantle of God, and of itself your soul will be transported to the Bosom and Source of eternal beauty and will sing the song of triumph, casting itself down with the Seraphim before the eternal throne of the Most High."

While the triumphant singing of the Song of the Seraphim resounds in the temple, the deacon stands in the altar before the Holy Gifts from which the aer and veils have been removed and waves the ripidion above them so that nothing may touch them or fall into the holy chalice. Meanwhile, the priest secretly prays this prayer:

With these blessed hosts, O Master, Lover of mankind, we also cry aloud and say: Holy art Thou and most holy, Thou, and Thine Only-begotten Son, and Thy Holy Spirit; holy art Thou and most holy, and majestic is Thy glory, O Thou Who so loved Thy world that Thou gavest Thine Only-begotten Son, that whosoever believeth in Him should not perish, but have everlasting life; Who, when He had come and fulfilled all the dispensation for us, on the night in which He was betrayed, or rather gave Himself up for the life of the world, took bread in His holy and most pure and unblemished hands, and when He had given thanks, and had blessed it, and hallowed it, and broken it, He gave it to His holy disciples and apostles, saying: (DLJC pp. 143–145)

After this the priest exclaims:

Take, eat. This is My Body, which is broken for you for the remission of sins. (DLJC p. 145)

The deacon follows these words of the priest by silently pointing to the holy bread with the three fingers with which he holds his orarion. The choir solemnly responds: **Amen** (DLJC p. 145). After the priest says softly:

And likewise the cup after supper, saying: (DLJC p. 145)

he then pronounces the words of the Saviour Himself aloud:

Drink of it, all of you. This is My Blood of the New Testament, which is shed for you and for many, for the remission of sins. (DLJC p. 145)

Again the deacon follows the exclamation of the priest by reverently pointing to the holy chalice with the three fingers with which he holds the orarion, and the choir responds: **Amen** (DLJC p. 145). The congregation attends to the holy words issuing from the altar as to the words of the Saviour Himself. Now comes the moment of the elevation. The altar is no longer the upper room, the holy table no longer a table; it is the place of sacrifice, that Golgotha where the Son of God offered Himself as a sacrifice for us.

The priest prays silently:

Having called to remembrance this saving command-ment and all those things which came to pass for us: the cross, the grave, the resurrection on the third day, the

ascension into the heavens, the sitting at the right hand, the second and glorious coming again, (DLJC p. 147)

and then he exclaims aloud:

Thine own of Thine own, we offer unto Thee, in behalf of all, and for all. (DLJC p. 147)

At this moment, while the choirs are singing that soft and touching hymn:

We praise Thee, we bless Thee, we give thanks to Thee, O Lord, and we pray to Thee, O our God, (DLJC p. 147)

inside the altar the most dread and most mysterious action in the whole Liturgy takes place. What is offered as a sacrifice to the Creator becomes actually the very sacrifice which our Redeemer offered on Golgotha for all men. The bread and wine that hitherto have been only symbols of Christ's Body and Blood become the actual Body and Blood of Christ. In the altar, a threefold invocation to the Holy Spirit takes place:

O Lord, Who didst send down Thy Most-holy Spirit at the third hour upon Thine apostles: Take Him not from us, O Good One, but renew Him in us who pray unto Thee. (DLJC p. 149)

Immediately after the first invocation, the deacon softly says the verse:

Create in me a clean heart, O God, and renew a right spirit within me. (DLJC p. 149)

Immediately after the second invocation, he reads:

Cast me not away from Thy presence, and take not Thy Holy Spirit from me. (DLJC p. 149)

After the third invocation, the deacon bows his head and points to the holy bread with his orarion and without daring to utter a word himself, he says from the depths of his soul:

Bless, master, the Holy Bread. (DLJC p. 149)

The priest makes the sign of the cross over the bread with the prayer of the consummation of the sacrament of the Eucharist. The deacon says: **Amen** (DLJC p. 149). Reverently the deacon points with his orarion to the holy chalice and says:

Bless, master, the Holy Cup. (DLJC p. 149)

While blessing it, the priest says the same prayer over the chalice. After the sign of the cross has been made over it, the deacon says: **Amen** (DLJC p. 149). And pointing to the chalice and diskos together, the deacon says from the depths of his heart:

Bless them both, master. (DLJC p. 151)

And the priest blesses both, saying:

Changing them by Thy Holy Spirit.

The deacon exclaims: **Amen. Amen. Amen.** (DLJC p. 151).

The change has occurred. The very Body in which the Eternal Word was clothed when He was on earth, the Body of the Lord Himself now lies slain on the holy table, and the immolation has been accomplished by a word instead of a sword. Let everyone at this time forget the priest. It is not the priest, who in form and name is like ourselves, but it is the Supreme, Eternal High Priest Himself Who has accomplished this sacrifice, which He accomplishes eternally through His priests. On the holy table there lies not the symbol, not the appearance of the Body, but the actual Body of the Lord Who suffered on earth, endured blows, was spat on, was crucified, and buried, rose and ascended to heaven, and sits at the right hand of the Father.

From the belfry, the bell rings so that this sad moment may be proclaimed everywhere, wherever anyone can hear the bell, whether he is a pilgrim on the road, or a farmer tilling his land, or a person sitting at home or occupied elsewhere, or languishing in prison, or seriously ill in bed—so that wherever he is, at this moment he may send up prayer to the Lord for the salvation of his soul and pray that this dread mystery may not be for the judgment and condemnation of any of his brothers.

All the worshippers in the temple at this moment throw themselves down before the Lord and the celebrants also prostrate themselves before the holy table and make fervent bows. At this great moment, everyone praying in the church lifts up his inner voice to the Lord that He may remember him in His kingdom. The deacon bows his head to the priest and says:

Remember me, a sinner, holy master. (DLJC p. 151)

And the priest responds:

May the Lord God remember thee in His kingdom, always, now and ever, and unto the ages of ages. (DLJC p. 151)

The deacon says: **Amen** (DLJC p. 151), and takes his place to the right of the holy table, fanning with the ripidion as though with the wings of the Seraphim above the Holy Gifts. Meanwhile, the priest prays secretly that the Body and Blood of Christ, which are present on the holy table, may be for the sobriety of soul, for the forgiveness of sins, for communion with the Holy Spirit, for the fulfillment of the kingdom of heaven, for confidence towards God, but not for judgment or condemnation. Then he remembers all before the Lord, in the presence of His very Body and Blood, and he collects before Christ His whole Church— those who are still struggling on earth and those dwelling in heaven, recalling all, from the Patriarchs and Prophets of the Old Testament down to each of the Christians now living. Before all others, he mentions especially the most holy Mother of God, and in response to this and in her honor the choir sings a hymn of praise to her which the whole church repeats silently:

> **It is truly meet to bless thee, the Theotokos, ever-blessed and most blameless, and Mother of our God. More honorable than the Cherubim, and beyond compare more glorious than the Seraphim, who without corruption gavest birth to God the Word, the very Theotokos, thee do we magnify.** (DLJC p. 153)

After that, in the presence of the Body and Blood of the Lord, the priest mentions John the Forerunner, the Apostles, the saint whose memory is kept on that day, and all the saints, and he prays for all who have fallen asleep in the hope of resurrection to eternal life.

Then the priest mentions all the living, commencing with those placed in authority over others, whose calling is the highest, whose duties are the most difficult, and whose responsibility is the most terrifying. In the presence of the Lord's Body and Blood, he prays for the emperor, and reflecting on the holiness of his calling and the difficulty of his office, he prays fervently to God that He may strengthen him with His holy power, that He may cast down everything that may become an obstacle to his path to goodness, that He may subdue under his feet every enemy and adversary. And the priest prays that in a united effort for good the entire ship of state may respond to him, and that all the parts of this great structure (the civil authorities, the army) may honestly and firmly carry out their sacred duty, so that his reign may be peaceful:

> **Grant them, O Lord, peaceful governance, that in their calm we also may lead a quiet and peaceful life in all piety and purity.** (DLJC p. 155)

During this silent prayer in the altar, everyone present should pray for the same things and should pray vigorously and fervently as though praying for his own affairs and for his own soul, which is the most precious thing a man has.

The priest continues in prayer. He prays fervently for the preservation of those who have the highest spiritual rank and are consecrated to the guiding of the Church's helm, who must dispense the very word of God's truth. Considering how sacred their duty is and how grave their responsibility, the priest in contrition of heart offers these words to God:

> **. . . whom do Thou grant unto Thy holy churches in peace, safety, honor, health and length of days, rightly dividing the word of Thy truth.** (DLJC p. 157)

All the people present pray that those mentioned may be persons who are fit to teach aright the word of truth and in their rule proclaim the One God. Then the choir sings solemnly:

And each and every one. (DLJC p. 157)

The priest then prays for everyone and everything, beginning with the city and church in which the people present are praying, and embracing in his prayer all cities and lands and the faithful who live there, those who travel by sea and by land, the sick and suffering, and prisoners and their salvation. He prays for those who serve and bear fruit in the holy Churches, and for those who remember the poor. In the Liturgy of St Basil the Great, he prays for all men, in whatever state or condition they may be; for those who do good, that they may be strengthened still more in good; and for evildoers, that they may cease to do evil and, having offered sincere repentance, with their whole heart may turn to what is good. And especially he prays for all those whom he has been requested to remember on that day. Finally he prays for those whom he has forgotten to mention in his prayer.

In union with this secret prayer of their pastor, all the people pray silently for all persons and all things, each one adding at this moment the names of those known to him, not only those who love him but also those who do not love him—in fact, he prays for everyone. When this prayer of all for all has ended and the choir has finished singing:

And each and every one, (DLJC p. 157)

then the priest says aloud:

And grant unto us that with one mouth and one heart we may glorify and hymn Thy most honorable and majestic name: of the Father, and of the Son and of the Holy Spirit, now and ever, and to the ages of ages. (DLJC p. 159)

And thirsting for this union with all their hearts, the whole church responds with an affirmative **Amen** (DLJC p. 159), and is at this moment one, an undivided unity. **Amen** (DLJC p. 159), says everyone in his heart, knowing that just as there is one Church in heaven and on earth, one Faith and one Baptism, so in exactly the same way we who are united by the bond of love should be in harmony as brothers in the temple, like one body and one spirit. From the altar, the priest sends a gracious wish to all:

And may the mercies of our great God and our Saviour Jesus Christ be with you all. (DLJC p. 159)

The response:

And with thy spirit. (DLJC p. 159)

This concludes the holy prayers for all who form the Church of Christ, offered in the presence of His very Body and Blood.

The deacon goes to the ambo to recite the prayers for the actual Gifts[1] that have been offered to God, that they may not be for our judgment and condemnation. Raising the orarion with three fingers of his right hand, he urges all to pray:

Having called to remembrance all the Saints, again and again, in peace, let us pray to the Lord. (DLJC p. 159)

The choir sings:

Lord, have mercy.
For the precious Gifts offered and sanctified, let us pray to the Lord. (DLJC p. 159)

The choir sings:

Lord, have mercy. (DLJC p. 159)

The deacon calls:

That our God, the Lover of mankind, having accepted them upon His holy and most heavenly and noetic altar as an odor of spiritual fragrance, will send down upon us divine grace and the gift of the Holy Spirit, let us pray. (DLJC pp. 159–161)

The choir sings:

Lord, have mercy.
That we may be delivered from all tribulation, wrath and necessity, let us pray to the Lord. (DLJC p. 161)

The choir sings:

> **Lord, have mercy.**
> **Help us, have mercy on us, and keep us, O God, by Thy grace.** (DLJC p. 161)

The choir sings:

> **Lord, have mercy.**
> **That the whole day may be perfect, holy, peaceful, and sinless, let us ask of the Lord.** (DLJC p. 161)

And the choir sings:

> **Grant this, O Lord.**
> **An angel of peace, a faithful guide, a guardian of our souls and bodies, let us ask of the Lord.** (DLJC p. 163)

The choir sings:

> **Grant this, O Lord.**
> **Pardon and remission of our sins and offenses, let us ask of the Lord.** (DLJC p. 163)

The choir sings:

> **Grant this, O Lord.** (DLJC p. 163)

Now the deacon, no longer appealing to the saints for help but turning to the Lord Himself, says:

Things good and profitable for our souls, and peace for the world, let us ask of the Lord. (DLJC p. 163)

The choir sings:

Grant this, O Lord.
That we may complete the remaining time of our life in peace and repentance, let us ask of the Lord. (DLJC p. 163)

The choir sings:

Grant this, O Lord.
A Christian ending to our life, painless, blameless, peaceful, and a good defense before the dread judgment seat of Christ, let us ask. (DLJC p. 163)

The choir sings:

Grant this, O Lord.
Having asked for the unity of the faith and the communion of the Holy Spirit, let us commit ourselves and one another and all our life unto Christ, our God. (DLJC pp. 163–165)

And all sing in complete surrender:

To Thee, O Lord. (DLJC p. 165)

But instead of the doxology to the Holy Trinity,[2] the priest says:

And vouchsafe us, O Master, that with boldness and without condemnation we may dare to call upon Thee the heavenly God as Father, and to say: (DLJC p. 165)

At this moment, all the faithful, no longer as servants filled with fear but as children, as innocent babes, should be led by the prayers and the whole service and by the gradual progress of holy rites to that heavenly compunction, that angelic state of soul in which man can speak directly to God, as the gentlest father and can thus sing the Lord's Prayer:

Our Father, Who art in the heavens, hallowed be Thy Name. Thy kingdom come, Thy will be done, on earth, as it is in heaven. Give us this day our daily bread, and forgive us our debts, as we forgive our debtors; and lead us not into temptation, but deliver us from the evil one. (DLJC p. 165)

Everything is embraced in this prayer, and it includes everything we need. In the petition: **Hallowed be Thy name** (DLJC p. 165), we pray for what we must pray for before everything else. Wherever God's name is hallowed is a good place for everyone, where all live in love, for God's name is sanctified only through love.

By the words: **Thy kingdom come** (DLJC p. 165), the realm of justice is invoked upon earth, for without the coming of God there is no justice, since God is justice.

Faith and reason lead man to the words: **Thy will be done** (DLJC p. 165). What will can be lovelier or more holy than God's? Who knows better than the Creator Himself what His creation needs? Whom can we trust more than Him Who is all beneficent goodness and perfection?

By the words: **Give us this day our daily bread** (DLJC p. 165), we ask for all that is needful for our daily existence, both spiritual and physical. Our spiritual bread is God's Wisdom, Christ Himself, Who said:

> **I am the living bread which came down from heaven. If anyone eats of this bread, he will live forever. John 6:51**

By the words: **And forgive us our debts** (DLJC p. 165), we ask that all our sins, which weigh us down, may be taken from us. We ask that we may be forgiven everything that we owe our Creator, who daily and hourly stretches out His hand to us in the persons of our brothers, imploring compassion and mercy.

By the words: **Lead us not into temptation** (DLJC p. 165), we pray for deliverance from all that troubles our spirit and deprives us of peace of soul.

By the words: **But deliver us from the evil one** (DLJC p. 165), we pray for the joy of heaven. For as soon as the evil one leaves us, at once joy enters our soul and though on earth it is as though we were in heaven.

Thus this prayer, which the very Wisdom of God has taught us to pray, embraces and includes everything. And to whom must we pray? To the Father of Wisdom. And since all present ought to repeat this prayer not only with their lips but also with the inward sighs of their pure, innocent and childlike hearts, so the singing of it by the choir ought to be childlike. This prayer should be sung not in loud and severe tones but with soft, clear, childlike voices, as though kissing the soul, so that the spring like breath of heaven may be felt in it, that the kisses of the angels may be borne in it; for in this prayer we no longer call our Creator "God" but we address Him as **our Father** (DLJC p. 165).

At the end of this prayer, the priest from the altar greets all as though with the greeting of our Saviour: **Peace be unto all** (DLJC p. 165). They reply to him: **And to thy spirit** (DLJC p. 167). But with the words: **Bow your heads unto the Lord** (DLJC p. 167), the deacon reminds us of the inner confession of the heart that everyone should make within himself. At this time, the priest prays at the holy table for everyone:

> **We give thanks unto Thee, O King invisible, Who by Thine immeasurable might hast created all things, and in the multitude of Thy mercies hast brought all things from nonbeing into being; do Thou Thyself, O Master, look down from heaven upon them that have bowed their heads unto Thee, for they have not bowed down unto flesh and blood, but unto Thee, the awesome God. Do Thou, therefore, O Master, distribute these Things here set forth unto us all for good, according to the need**

of each; sail with them that voyage, travel with them that journey, heal the sick, O Thou Physician of our souls and bodies. (DLJC p. 167)

Immediately afterwards, he says aloud this wonderful praise of the Trinity, addressed to the heavenly mercy of God:

Through the grace and compassions and love for mankind of Thine Only-begotten Son, with Whom Thou art blessed, together with Thine Most-holy and good and life-creating Spirit, now and ever, and to the ages of ages. (DLJC p. 167)

The choir sings: **Amen.** The priest, preparing to communicate himself and afterwards the people with the Body and Blood of Christ, prays this secret prayer:

Attend, O Lord Jesus Christ our God, out of Thy holy dwelling- place and from the glorious throne of Thy kingdom, and come and sanctify us, O Thou that sittest with the Father on high, and invisibly abidest here with us; and vouchsafe by Thy strong right hand to impart unto us Thy most pure Body and precious Blood, and through us to all the people. (DLJC p. 169)

Here the deacon, who during the singing of "Our Father" stands on the ambo in front of the holy doors and girds himself with his orarion by binding it in the form of a cross like the angels who fold their wings crosswise and cover their faces with them before the unapproachable light of the Godhead, bows thrice, as does the priest, and says silently:

O God, cleanse me, a sinner, and have mercy on me.
(DLJC p. 169)

Then with the exclamation: **Let us attend** (DLJC p. 169), he calls upon all to be attentive. The altar is closed to the view of the people, the curtain is drawn, so that the priests may first take Communion. From the depths of the altar resounds the voice of the priest who elevates the holy "Lamb" and says:

Holy Things are for the holy. (DLJC p. 169)

The whole congregation of the faithful trembles at these words, which proclaim that one must be holy in order to receive holiness. They respond:

One is holy, one is Lord, Jesus Christ, to the glory of God the Father. Amen. (DLJC p. 169)

The deacon goes into the altar to commune. After that, the Communion Hymn is sung, that is, a verse selected from the Psalms and appropriate to the day.

The priest now breaks the holy Lamb, according to the sign made at the proskomedia, crosswise into four parts, saying reverently:

**Broken and distributed is the Lamb of God; broken yet
not divided; ever eaten, though never consumed, but
sanctifying them that partake thereof.** (DLJC p. 171)

He places the first part in the chalice with the most pure
Blood, the second he lays aside for his own and the deacon's Communion in the form unmixed with the Blood.
He divides the other parts according to the number of communicants, yet in this dividing he does not divide the actual
Body of Christ and in the smallest particle the same whole
Christ remains—just as in every member of our body the
same human soul is present, not as a part of itself but whole
and undivided; and as in a mirror, even if it is broken into
a hundred pieces, the reflection of the same objects is pre-
served even in the smallest piece; and just as sound that
reaches us preserves its unity and remains the same single,
complete sound even if heard by a thousand ears.

All the portions removed at the proskomedia in honor
of the saints, in memory of the departed and in commemoration of the living, are not yet placed in the chalice, but
for the time being they remain on the diskos, because the
Church uses for Communion only the portions that con-
stitute the Body and Blood of Christ.

In the early days of the Church, the people partook of
the separate elements just as the clergy commune now,
and everyone received in his hands the most pure Body of
our Lord and then drank the most pure Blood from the
chalice. But when newly converted Christians, Christians
only in name, began to carry away the Holy Gifts to their

homes to use them for superstitious or magical purposes or behaved in a disorderly manner in church, pushing one another and making noise and confusion, then St John Chrysostom ordered the people no longer to receive Holy Communion separately but in the mixed form, and that It should not be given to the people in their hands, but in a holy spoon, which serves as a figure of the tongs with which the fiery Seraphim touched the lips of the Prophet Isaiah. Thus everyone is reminded of the significance of the mystery that touches their lips.

After communing first himself and then the deacon, the servant of Christ becomes a new man, cleansed by Holy Communion from all his sins, truly holy at this moment and worthy to commune others. The holy doors are opened, announcing by their opening the opening of the kingdom of heaven itself, which Christ won for all by offering Himself as the saving food for the whole world. The deacon says in a solemn voice:

With fear of God and with faith draw nigh. (DLJC p. 183)

In the form of the holy chalice, which the deacon brings out as he says these words, is represented the appearance of the Risen Christ and His coming out to the people to bring them all with Himself into His Father's house. And like a transfigured Seraphim, the priest stands in the holy doors with the chalice in his hands. With the thunder of triumphant singing the whole choir replies to the deacon:

Blessed is He that cometh in the name of the Lord. God is the Lord, and hath appeared unto us. (DLJC p. 183)

And with the thunder of this spiritual song coming from the depths of a renewed spirit, the whole church sings with the choir.

Flaming with longing for God, burning with the fire of holy love for Him, with their hands folded crosswise over their hearts, the communicants approach one after other, and with bowed head each repeats to himself this confession of faith in the Crucified[3]:

I believe, O Lord, and I confess that Thou art truly the Christ, the Son of the living God, Who didst come into the world to save sinners of whom I am chief. Moreover, I believe that this is truly Thy most pure Body, and that this is truly Thine Own precious Blood. Wherefore, I pray Thee: Have mercy on me and forgive me my transgressions, voluntary and involuntary, in word and deed, in knowledge and in ignorance. And vouchsafe me to partake without condemnation of Thy most pure Mysteries unto the remission of sins and life everlasting. Amen. (DLJC p. 177)

After pausing for a moment to grasp with his mind the significance of what he is approaching, he continues from the depths of his heart to repeat the words that follow:

Of Thy Mystical Supper, O Son of God, receive me today as a communicant; for I will not speak of the Mystery to Thine enemies, nor will I give Thee a kiss as did Judas, but like the Thief do I confess Thee: Remember me, O Lord, in Thy kingdom. (DLJC p. 179)

And after a moment's reverent silence, he continues:

Let not the communion of Thy holy Mysteries be unto me for judgment or condemnation, O Lord, but for healing of soul and body. (DLJC p. 179)

After saying this confession, each one goes up not to the priest but to the fiery Seraphim, preparing himself with open lips to receive from the holy spoon the fiery coal of the Body and Blood of the Lord, which will burn away all his sins like thorns. When the priest has raised the holy spoon to his lips and called him by name, saying:

The servant of God [name] partaketh of the precious and holy Body and Blood of our Lord God and Saviour Jesus Christ, unto the remission of sins and life everlasting, (DLJC p. 185)

he receives the Body and Blood of the Lord. His lips are wiped with the communion veil, while the words of the Seraphim to the Prophet Isaiah are repeated:

Behold, this hath touched my lips, and taketh away mine iniquities, and purgeth away my sins. Isa 6:7

Christ has come down with His Body and entered his interior like as into a coffin so that, having penetrated the secret treasury of his heart, He may rise up in his spirit and accomplish there His burial as well as His resurrection. Shining with the light of this spiritual resurrection, the Church repeats by the lips of her sacred ministers this exultant song:

Having beheld the resurrection of Christ, let us worship the holy Lord Jesus, the Only Sinless One. We worship Thy Cross, O Christ, and Thy holy Resurrection we hymn and glorify; for Thou art our God, and we know none other beside Thee; we call upon Thy Name. O come, all you faithful, let us worship Christ's holy Resurrection, for behold, through the Cross joy hath come to all the world. Ever blessing the Lord, we hymn His Resurrection, for having endured crucifixion, He hath destroyed death by death. (DLJC p. 185)

Shine, shine, O new Jerusalem, for the glory of the Lord is risen upon thee; dance now, and be glad, O Sion; and do thou exult, O pure Theotokos, in the arising of Him Whom thou didst bear. (DLJC p. 187)

O great and most sacred Pascha, Christ! O Wisdom, and Word of God, and Power! Grant us more perfectly to partake of Thee, in the unwaning day of Thy kingdom. (DLJC p. 187)

After the Gifts are placed on the altar, all the particles which have been left on the diskos and had been taken out in memory of the saints, for the repose of the departed, and for the spiritual health of the living, are now immersed in the holy chalice. In this act of immersion, the whole Church communes of the Body and Blood of Christ, both the pilgrim and militant Church on earth and the Church Triumphant in heaven. The Mother of God, the Prophets and Apostles, Church Fathers, hierarchs, solitaries, martyrs, all sinners for whom particles were removed, those living on earth and the departed, commune at this moment of the Body and Blood of Christ. And the priest, standing before God at this moment as the representative of His whole Church, prays for all, that their sins may be washed away in His precious Blood. For the sacrifice was offered by Christ for the redemption of all, equally for those who lived before His coming and for those who lived after it. And however sinful his prayer may be, the priest offers it for all, even for the very holiest, for as St Chrysostom says, the general purification of the universe has to take place.

After covering the chalice and diskos, the priest says the prayer of thanksgiving to our Lord, the Benefactor of our souls, for having granted him to partake of His heavenly and immortal mysteries, concluding with a petition that He may guide our way and strengthen us all in His holy fear, guard our life and make our steps sure.

Turning to the people, the priest blesses them with the words

Save, O God, Thy people, and bless Thine inheritance.
(DLJC p. 187)

For he assumes that everyone because of his purity at this moment has become an heir of God. Then he turns mentally to the Lord's ascension with which He concluded His sojourn on earth. With the deacon, he stands before the altar, bows, censes for the last time, and during the censing he says silently:

Be Thou exalted above the heavens, O God, and Thy glory above all the earth. (DLJC p. 187)

Meanwhile, with triumphant singing and with voices exultant with spiritual gladness, the choir incites the enlightened souls of all present to pronounce after it these words of spiritual joy:

We have seen the true Light, we have received the Heavenly Spirit, we have found the True Faith. We worship the undivided Trinity, Who hath saved us. (DLJC p. 187)

The deacon appears in the holy doors with the diskos on his head but does not say a single word. Immediately after the deacon, the priest appears with the holy chalice, representing the Lord's ascension and proclaiming that our Lord Who has ascended into heaven will be with us on earth till the end of time with the words:

Always, now and ever, and unto the ages of ages. (DLJC p. 189)

Then the chalice and diskos are taken back to the table of oblation on which the proskomedia was performed, and which is no longer the manger—the place of Christ's birth—but now represents that upper region of glory to which the Son of God ascended after accomplishing the salvation of mankind.

Here the whole church, led by the choir, unites its prayer in one triumphant song of thanksgiving, and these are its words of praise:

Let our mouth be filled with Thy praise, O Lord, that we may hymn Thy glory, for Thou hast vouchsafed us to partake of Thy holy, divine, immortal and life-giving Mysteries. Keep us in Thy holiness, that we may meditate on Thy righteousness all the day long. (DLJC p. 189)

And the choir then sings thrice: **Alleluia** (DLJC p. 189), which tells of the unceasing work and omnipresence of God. The deacon goes to the ambo to urge those present for the last time to pray with thanksgiving. Holding up his orarion with three fingers, he says:

Aright! Having partaken of the divine, holy, most pure, immortal, heavenly, and life-giving, fearful Mysteries of Christ, let us worthily give thanks unto the Lord. (DLJC p. 191)

And giving thanks in their hearts, all sing softly: **Lord, have mercy** (DLJC p. 191).

Help us, save us, have mercy on us, and keep us, O God, by Thy grace. (DLJC p. 191)

calls the deacon for the last time, and all sing: **Lord, have mercy** (DLJC p. 191).

Having asked that the whole day may be perfect, holy, peaceful and sinless, let us commit ourselves and one another, and all our life to Christ, our God. (DLJC p. 191)

With the obedience of a gentle child and with filial trust in God, all cry:

To Thee, O Lord. (DLJC p. 191)

The priest, who has meanwhile folded the antimension and has made the sign of the cross over it with the Book of the Gospels, pronounces the doxology to the Trinity, Who has enlightened the whole course of the service like a lighthouse and now with still more powerful light illumines our enlightened souls. And this time the Trinitarian doxology takes this form:

For Thou art our sanctification, and unto Thee do we send up glory, to the Father, and to the Son, and to the

Holy Spirit, now and ever, and to the ages of ages. (DLJC
p. 191)

The Church bids us offer common prayer on behalf of
all. We do not learn the deep meaning of such prayer and
its strict necessity from the wise of this world, nor from the
critics of our times, but rather from those exalted persons
who through high spiritual perfection and a heavenly or
angelic life attained to a knowledge of the deepest spiritual mysteries and clearly saw that amongst those who live
in God there is no separation; that relationships are not
broken by the corruption of our body; that love reaches
its highest measure in heaven, its home; that a brother
who goes from us becomes still closer to us through the
power of love; and that everything that comes from Christ
is eternal, because its Source is Himself eternal. They have
also become aware with the organs of their senses that
even in heaven a triumphant Church prays for her brothers who are pilgrims on earth. They have realized that
God has prepared for them the highest of blessings—that
bliss of prayer. For God does nothing and shows no benefit without letting His creatures share both in the doing
of it and in the benefit, so that they may enjoy the highest
joy of well-doing. The angel delivers His command and
is blessed in doing so. The Seraphim extols His infinite
beauty and is blessed in the process. The saint in heaven
prays for his brothers on earth and is blessed because he
prays. And everyone shares with God in all His highest
joys. Millions of the most perfect beings go out from the

hand of God to share in His highest blessings, and there is no end of them, since there is no end to God's blessings.

After this, the priest gives the benediction from the holy doors:

The blessing of the Lord be upon you, through His grace and love for mankind, always, now and ever, and to the ages of ages. (DLJC p. 195)

The choir sings: **Amen** (DLJC p. 197).

The priest brings the altar bread, from which the portions were cut out and removed, to the people, and through this we remember the great and ancient agape or love-feast that was observed by the Christians of early times. Therefore, everyone who receives a prosphoron ought to take it as bread from the feast at which the Creator of the world Himself has spoken with His people, and one ought to consume it reverently, thinking of all men as one's dearest and most tender brothers. And as was the custom in the early Church, one ought to eat the prosphoron before all other foods or take it home to one's family or send it to the sick or the poor or to those who have not been able to attend the Liturgy.

After distributing the holy bread, the priest blesses all the people and reads the dismissal of the Holy Liturgy with the words:

May Christ our true God, through the intercessions of His most-pure Mother; [and the rest]; of our father among

the saints John Chrysostom, archbishop of Constantinople; of Saint [names: whose temple it is and whose day it is] and of all the Saints, have mercy on us and save us, for He is good and the Lover of mankind. (DLJC p. 197)

Having been blessed by the cross and having venerated it, the people disperse while the choir sings "Many Years" for the imperial and ruling house, the Holy Synod, and all Orthodox Christians.

The priest removes his vestments in the sanctuary, saying:

Now lettest Thou Thy servant depart in peace, O Master, according to Thy word; for mine eyes have seen Thy salvation, which Thou hast prepared before the face of all peoples, the light of revelation for the Gentiles, and the glory of Thy people Israel. Luke 2:29–32

He accompanies the unvesting with the troparion in praise of the Father and Hierarch of the Church whose Liturgy was celebrated and concludes with a prayer of praise to the most pure and holy Virgin:

More honorable than the Cherubim, and beyond compare more glorious than the Seraphim, who without corruption gavest birth to God the Word, the very Theotokos, thee do we magnify. Glory to the Father, the Son and the Holy Spirit, now and ever, and to the ages of ages. Amen. (from "Prayers after Holy Communion," *Prayer Book* [Jordanville, N.Y.: Holy Trinity Monastery, 2003])

Meanwhile the deacon consumes all that remains in the chalice. He pours wine and water into it, and having washed its inner walls, he drinks what remains and carefully dries the chalice with the sponge so that nothing is left. Then he puts the sacred vessels together, covers and ties them, and says as the priest earlier:

Now lettest Thou Thy servant ... (DLJC p. 201)

and repeats the same hymns and prayers. Finally they both leave the church, bearing radiant freshness in their faces, exultant joy in their hearts, and thanksgiving to the Lord on their lips.

CONCLUSION

The effect of the Divine Liturgy is great. It is celebrated openly and visibly before the eyes of the entire world, and yet it is full of mystery. If the worshipper follows every action reverently and diligently, his soul attains a high state, the commandments of Christ become possible for him, Christ's yoke becomes easy and His burden light. After leaving the temple in which he has attended the divine love-feast, he looks upon all men as his brothers. Whether he resumes his customary tasks in business or in his family or wherever he may be, he involuntarily preserves in his soul the high resolve of such association with people as is inspired by the love brought from heaven by the God-Man.

If he has authority over others, he will involuntarily become more merciful towards his subordinates. If he himself is under the authority of another, he will obey him willingly and with love. If he sees someone asking for help, his heart will be more inclined than at other times to assist him. If he is poor, he will gratefully accept the smallest gift, and he will never pray for his benefactor with such thankfulness as at this time. And all who have attentively followed the Divine Liturgy depart the church gentler, kinder in their relations with others, friendlier, quieter in all their actions. Therefore, it is imperative for anyone wishing to succeed in the spiritual life to attend the Divine Liturgy as often as possible and follow it attentively. Imperceptibly it molds and forms a person, and if society has not completely gone to pieces and if people do not yet breathe irreconcilable hate towards one another, the hidden reason behind it all is the Divine Liturgy, which reminds a person to cherish holy, heavenly love towards his brother. Therefore, if one wants to strengthen himself in love, one should go as often as possible with fear, faith, and love to the holy table of love. And if he feels he is unworthy to receive God Himself, Who is Love, into his mouth, at least he should be a witness when others commune, so that imperceptibly and indiscernibly, he may become more perfect after each liturgy.

The influence of the Divine Liturgy can be great and incalculable if a person makes it a rule to apply in life what he has heard there. Teaching all equally, benefiting equally people of all social conditions and professions, from the emperor down to the poorest beggar, the Liturgy says one thing in one language to everyone. It teaches love, which is the bond of all fellowship, the hidden spring of everything that keeps all life in rhythmic motion.

But if the Divine Liturgy affects so powerfully those who are present at its celebration, it acts still more strongly on the celebrant or priest. If he celebrates reverently, with fear and faith and love, he is purified and like a sacred vessel remains pure for the whole of that day. In the performance of his numerous pastoral duties, in his family, among his relatives or his parishioners, who are also his family, he represents the Saviour Himself. In all his actions Christ will act and in his words Christ will speak.

Whether he uses his influence to reconcile those who are quarrelling, to move the strong to have mercy on the weak, to make the hard-hearted gentler, to comfort the grieved, to encourage the oppressed to have patience— the priest's words have the power of healing oil, and in every place they will be words of peace and love.

APPENDIX

A Short Life and Appraisal of N. V. Gogol

N. V. Gogol is known as one of the great geniuses of both Russian and world literature. His significance to the history of the Russian Orthodox Church is less well understood. The religious aspect of his character was hidden for a very long time, both from his contemporaries and subsequent generations.

Nikolai Vasilievich Gogol was born on March 20, 1809, in a small village within the Poltava gubernia. It was a beautiful and captivating corner of the Ukrainian countryside where he lived until the age of twelve. As a child, he was prone to sickness and had an impressionable nature. His father, Vasilii Afanasievich, was of ancient Ukrainian noble descent and was a talented author in his own right. He was known both as a storyteller and a great lover of the Church, being drawn particularly to its ritual and singing. Gogol's great-grandfather was a priest, and both his grandfather and father were educated at the Kiev Spiritual Academy.

From an early age, Gogol struggled with depression. He wrote to his mother in 1829: "I often think to myself, why did God, who created a unique (or at least a very rare), pure, fiery soul that longs for all that is exalted and beautiful, why did he dress all of it in such a frightful mess of contradictions, stubbornness, obnoxious self-will, and shameful self-abasement?" There were also many external influences on Gogol's spiritual development: nature, folk poetry, sentimental Romantic literature, and the theater.

His father died when Gogol was sixteen; his mother would outlive him. This early encounter with mortality spurred him to spiritual growth. He began to feel an impulse to break out of his "wretched anonymity" and to do something important "to give meaning to his existence in the world." He sought to achieve the first goal by dedicating himself to the law and through personal involvement in the social and civic life of his county.

After graduating from the Nezhinskii Lyceum in 1828, he moved to St Petersburg, where he struggled to find both work and a place to live. He turned to a manuscript he had written before his arrival in the capital and arranged for its publication under a pseudonym. The critics lambasted it and he took back nearly all the printed copies from booksellers and had them burned. After a period of aimless wandering in Germany, he returned to the Russian capital but was again unable to find work. Thus, he turned again to writing, this time with greater success after the publication of his first collection of short stories, *Evenings on a Farm near Dikanka*.

More success was to follow and in 1831 he was introduced to A. S. Pushkin. Under his influence, Gogol was inspired to understand the ultimate goal of his art as a service to humanity that had the character of a moral duty. Pushkin taught Gogol that "Poets are born for inspiration, for sweet sounds and prayer." When Pushkin died in 1837, Gogol wrote, ". . . all I treasured was his eternal and inviolable word. I did nothing, I wrote nothing without his counsel."

Gogol was equally influenced by another poet: Vasily Zhukovsky, who wrote, "Poetry is God in the holy dreams of the earth." From Zhukovsky, Gogol understood that religious truth, moral good, and the beauty of art are a trinity, a triune image of perfection. Nevertheless, he struggled to realize this vision in his own life, dependent as it was on his own inner spiritual growth and development.

Despite going on to receive critical acclaim for his play *The Inspector General*, Gogol continued to suffer from inner torments and decided to travel abroad again to "walk off his sorrow." He visited Switzerland, Germany, and Italy before returning to Russia to complete his novel *Dead Souls*. For nearly five years between 1842 –1847, he lived in Germany. Whilst there, he rekindled his interest in spiritual books. He ordered copies from Russia and read the works of the Holy Fathers, the *Philokalia*, the works of St Dmitry of Rostov, Bishop Innocent, Lazar Baranovich, Stefan Yavorsky, "Christian Teachings," and other spiritual journals. Lacking proper preparation and guidance for this, he began to imagine that he had achieved a high spiritual state, and thus embarked upon mandatory daily readings and ascetical labors. But beyond all the excesses, in the deepest parts of Gogol's unhappy soul smoldered a true and unwavering love for Christ, and many hidden, pure tears of genuine repentance fell to the ground, unseen by the world.

In 1850 and 1851, Gogol traveled to the Optina Hermitage and spoke with the elders Moses, Anthony, and Makary. These conversations had a good influence on his still tormented soul. Thus, at the end of 1851, he was able to carefully revise and finish writing *Meditations on the Divine Liturgy*. He had begun this in 1845 as a "creative testament" and wished to publish it in a cheap edition for the common people. It is one of his most inspired and profound writings—a simple, clear, and accessibly written commentary on the Orthodox liturgy.

At the beginning of 1852, Gogol was deeply shocked by the death of A. S. Khomiakov's wife, who was the sister of Gogol's friend, the poet Yazykov. During her memorial service, he cried out, "It is all finished for me." Two weeks later he had some kind of vision where he saw himself as dead. He received Unction and Holy Communion and began to prepare for death. Ten days later, on February 21, 1852, he died.

This article is largely extracted from the short work of Professor Ivan Andreev, *Gogol as a Religious Personality*, translated into English by Nicholas Kotar. It is available as a free PDF download on the website www.holytrinitypublications.com.

NOTES

THE OFFICE OF PREPARATION

1. The proskomedia is the service of the preparation of the gifts of bread and wine for the Divine Liturgy.

2. The word *altar* means the floor area east of the iconostasis, sometimes called the *bema* (sanctuary in Western usage). The term *holy table* means the table in the middle of the altar.

3. The double orarion worn by the priest is typically called an epitrachelion.

4. The third and sixth hours are normally read in church before the beginning of the Divine Liturgy whilst the proskomedia is taking place in the altar. The first hour is read at the conclusion of the All-Night Vigil, and the ninth hour before a vesperal Divine Liturgy is served.

THE LITURGY OF THE CATECHUMENS

1. The iconostasis is the screen that separates the altar from the main body of the church, on which are placed icons of Christ, the Mother of God, and the saints.

THE LITURGY OF THE FAITHFUL

1. Gifts: the bread and wine, now the Body and Blood of Christ.

2. At the end of a litany, there is normally an exclamation that includes some form of Trinitarian doxology. That is not the case here with the doxology being exclaimed after the Lord's Prayer is sung.

3. In contemporary Russian practice, this prayer and the two that follow are said audibly by the priest after he comes out of the altar with the chalice and before the people approach to receive communion.

SUBJECT INDEX

The citations in parentheses following the page numbers refer to note numbers; e.g., 101(n1) refers to the text associated with note 1 on page 101.

SCRIPTURE INDEX